The Silk Road

A Captivating Guide to the Ancient Network of Trade Routes Established during the Han Dynasty of China and How It Connected the East and West

© Copyright 2020

This document is geared towards providing exact and reliable information regarding the topic and issue covered. The publication is sold with the idea that the publisher is not required to render accounting, officially permitted, or otherwise qualified services. If advice is necessary, legal or professional, a practiced individual in the profession should be ordered.

From a Declaration of Principles which was accepted and approved equally by a Committee of the American Bar Association and a Committee of Publishers and Associations.

In no way is it legal to reproduce, duplicate, or transmit any part of this document in either electronic means or in printed format. Recording of this publication is strictly prohibited and any storage of this document is not allowed unless with written permission from the publisher. All rights reserved.

The information provided herein is stated to be truthful and consistent, in that any liability, in terms of inattention or otherwise, by any usage or abuse of any policies, processes, or directions contained within is the sole and utter responsibility of the recipient reader. Under no circumstances will any legal responsibility or blame be held against the publisher for any reparation, damages, or monetary loss due to the information herein, either directly or indirectly.

Respective authors own all copyrights not held by the publisher.

The information herein is offered for informational purposes solely and is universal as so. The presentation of the information is without a contract or any type of guarantee assurance.

The trademarks that are used are without any consent, and the publication of the trademark is without permission or backing by the trademark owner. All trademarks and brands within this book are for clarifying purposes only and are owned by the owners themselves, not affiliated with this document.

Contents

INTRODUCTION 1
CHAPTER 1 – ROME, SILK, AND ANCIENT GEOGRAPHY 8
CHAPTER 2 – HAN SILK PRODUCTION AND TRADE..............12
CHAPTER 3 – THE KINGDOM OF LOULAN 17
CHAPTER 4 – BUDDHISTS ALONG THE SILK ROAD 22
CHAPTER 5 – TURFAN: AN OASIS ON THE SILK ROAD 26
CHAPTER 6 – THE LEGEND OF PRESTER JOHN........................30
CHAPTER 7 – GENGHIS KHAN, RULER OF THE WHOLE WORLD 34
CHAPTER 8 – THE LORD OF XANADU, KUBLAI KHAN: THE EMPEROR OF CHINA..47
CHAPTER 9 – MARCO POLO VISITS KUBLAI KHAN'S CHINA.................63
CHAPTER 10 – THE FINAL YEARS OF KUBLAI KHAN 77
CONCLUSION: THE DECLINE OF TRADE ALONG THE SILK ROAD....89
FURTHER READING 95

Introduction

Trade in goods necessarily carries with it trade in ideas. In other words, ideas piggy-back on the transmission of mercantile goods. It is through this means that religions, concepts of organization of societies, art, and material culture are transmitted from one society to another.

The development of civilizations and the enrichment of different cultures depend on trade between each other. Without trade and the transference of ideas, without vibrant cultures distinguished by religion and technology meeting with each other in the marketplace, civilizations fossilize and eventually decline. In some cases, they may even disappear. It is the impetus of the new that maintains the robust evolution of civilizations and cultures. Without new ideas impinging on them, civilizations and cultures are incapable of adapting to change and lose their vitality in an ever-changing world.

European civilizations and Asian civilizations, in particular, Chinese civilization, from roughly 100 BCE to 1450 CE, depended on interconnections through trade to evolve. This trade was carried out along what is known to us as the Silk Road.

The Silk Road, transformative for both Asian and European cultures and civilizations, owes its name and identity to modern scholars, among whom are archaeologists, linguists, economists, geographers, and historians. What we call the Silk Road today was actually named by the German explorer Ferdinand von Richthofen in 1877. He identified the Silk Road (Seidenstrasse) as a continuous land route along which trade was carried out, beginning in the era of imperial Rome and the Han Dynasty in China (206 BCE–220 CE). Von Richthofen's travels and discoveries, as well as his readings of the 2nd-century texts of the Greek geographer Ptolemy and the 1st-century writings of the Roman Pliny the Elder, convinced him that there was once a defined road from the Near East to central China along which silk was transported. According to von Richthofen, silk was the prime luxury good.

Von Richthofen's student, Swedish geographer Sven Hedin, undertook four expeditions to central Asia in the late 19th and early 20th centuries, mapping and observing the cultures of the various peoples he met along the way. His discoveries, in large measure, confirmed the notion that a Silk Road existed and that trade between the East and the West had been carried out for centuries in the distant past. Hedin reported on his travels in central Asia in multivolume technical reports. He summarized his research in a more popular book that made his work more accessible to the general public. This book, first published in Swedish in 1936 and was translated into English in 1938 under the title *The Silk Road*, inaugurated what was to become a worldwide fascination with the subject, a fascination that still persists today. Sven Hedin identified Chang'an (modern-day Xi'an), the Han dynasty capital, as the eastern end of the Silk Road, which he said terminated in the West some 7,000 kilometers (almost 4,350 miles) away in Antioch, Syria.

The idea of a Silk Road has, since the days of von Richthofen and Hedin, captured the imagination of the public. Starting in the 1960s, there was a flood of books, both scholarly and popular, published on the subject. The opening of China for archaeological research by non-Chinese scholars in the late 1970s increased public enthusiasm in the West as well. With the introduction of prohibitions against the plundering of archaeological sites, something that in the past had led to the dispersion of art and cultural treasures from China and central Asia to European and American museums, those who were enchanted by the idea of the Silk Road began to travel to previously out-of-bounds cities and towns situated along what was popularly known as the Silk Road. Interest in the trade route between the East and the West increased with the dissolution of the Soviet Union in 1991, as it opened up more Silk Road sites in Central Asia for study and exploration by tourists and scholars. The whole enterprise of study and exploitation of sites along the Silk Road has since became ensnared in the politics of bridging the histories of Eastern and Western civilizations. The notions of connecting the cultures of the East and the West has become a common topic in contemporary Silk Road studies. In recent years, the Eurocentric approach to world history has begun to crumble as more and more scholars from all regions of Asia have promoted a wider non-Eurocentric understanding of the histories of nations and cultures that once were of little interest in the West before.

The idea that exotic goods from the East, primarily silk, were transported thousands of miles across deserts and over mountains on long trains of camels, however picturesque and romantic, has proved to be untrue. With the increasing sophistication of archaeology and the interpretation of ancient texts by Eastern and Western scholars, a much more complicated picture of the Silk Road has emerged. It is now clear that the Silk Road was not a single, distinct avenue of trade but rather a complex series of paths connecting small communities and larger urban settlements in central Asia. Along these paths, objects of trade were moved by small caravans. So, contrary to popular belief, traders did not travel great distances. Objects from the East and the West were handed off from one middleman to another. Some goods did move all the way from central China to Rome, and later medieval Europe, but most of the trade was local, taking place between adjacent cultures or peoples. The variety of goods that moved short and long distances from the East to the West or vice versa were much more mundane than the silk that was thought to be so highly prized in the West. However, something that was not so mundane was the transmission of ideas along the trade routes that comprised the Silk Road. It was along this assortment of paths that religions, such as Buddhism, Islam, and Christianity, made inroads among the populations of central Asia and eventually China.

The enormous interest in the Silk Road has spawned a lively debate among researchers, whose numbers have increased exponentially with contributions from Chinese scholars and researchers in modern nations along the East-West trade routes. The globalization of academic work on the Silk Road is exemplified by the establishment of international centers for cooperative research, such as the Institute of Silk Road Studies in Kamakura, Japan, founded in 1990; the Central Asia-Caucasus Institute and Silk Road Studies Program, founded in Washington in 1996; and the Tang Centre for Silk Road Studies at the University of California, which was established in 2017. Among the research papers currently being published on the subject by these and other research centers, there is a notable abundance of scholarly articles questioning whether there was indeed a Silk Road. It has even been called "a romantic deception" and "the road that never was."

The concept of a singular Silk Road has been subject to revision, and it is now questioned whether East-West trade from Roman times to the 15th century involved much silk at all. Further, the notion of a single road has been replaced with the identification of a multiplicity of routes, which are more accurately called paths than roads. There is a great debate on which trade routes to include under the umbrella of the term "Silk Road." Some scholars are proponents of adding sea routes between south Asia and the West, and others conclude that the trade route from India through the Karakoram mountain range on the borders of Pakistan, India, and China cannot be excluded from Silk Road studies. Several contemporary scholars have also proposed that sea and land routes connecting Africa with the East belong in the realm of Silk Road studies.

The Silk Road, which has been understood as a generalized route of trade between the East and the West, is different from European, North African, and Near Eastern trade routes because until recently, it has been understood as solely being a land route; in fact, it was believed to be the longest overland trade route in human history. From pre-Roman times to the Railway Age in Europe, most of the trade within Europe was conducted by seas or rivers. Trade from the north to the south was facilitated by the existence of the long navigable rivers of Europe, such as the Danube, Rhine, and Volga, or by sea from the Mediterranean through the Atlantic Ocean to the North Sea and then the Baltic. European trade with North Africa and the Near East depended almost entirely on the Mediterranean Sea routes. Trade with India and beyond into Southeast Asia involved short overland transportation to centers where goods were transferred to ships plying the Indian Ocean. In contrast to this was the Silk Road, where vast stretches of often inhospitable land lay between trading entrepots. For this reason, it has captured the imagination of students of history, geography, and the transmission of culture.

Because the Silk Road was not a single path from China to the Near East but instead consisted of a network of shorter connected routes, the complexities of the terrain and cultures along the routes pose greater problems to understanding its history than trade routes that involved long-distance sea transportation. Near Eastern and Mediterranean ports are, by a straight line, 8,500 kilometers (almost 5,282 miles) distant from Xi'an, the ancient capital of China. The complicated topography of central Asia required traders to detour around impassable mountain ranges and traverse deserts from one oasis to another, as well as to contend with disruptions due to warfare between tribes and proto-nations. All of this would make the total distance between the East and the West much longer.

The routes of East/West trade were such that they encompassed a wide range of peoples or cultures that inhabited central Asia. These peoples lived in the modern nations of China, Kyrgyzstan, Tajikistan, Kazakhstan, Uzbekistan, Turkmenistan, Afghanistan, Iran, and Iraq.

Over the history of the Silk Road, the cultures that were involved in the movement of goods across central Asia changed as they were subject to invasions by displaced nomadic tribes and conquest by superior imperial powers. Thus, the complicated history of the Silk Road involves the history of peoples and geography that is better understood by local scholars and is, more often than not, completely beyond the knowledge of others outside the region. In effect, the understanding of the Silk Road among Europeans is almost as foggy as the Romans' comprehension of what lay in the East beyond the borders of their empire.

For the Europeans from Roman times to the 15th century and beyond, there existed a fascination for the exotic, unknown cultures and products of the East. From the evidence available, it seems as if there was not an equivalent fascination for Western culture among the Chinese. For the most part, the Chinese looked to the West, central Asia, and later as far as the Near East and Europe as a straightforward market for goods or, in short, a source of wealth.

European interest in the East can be traced back to the remarkable expansion of the Hellenistic Greek Empire under Alexander the Great. His military incursions into Asia, through Persia and modern-day Afghanistan, to the banks of the Indus River became the stuff of legend, and it drove Europeans to imagine the magnificence of mysterious Eastern civilizations. In expanding his empire to the East, Alexander planted outposts of Greek culture. These outposts or garrisons became centers for the transmission of ideas and goods of Eastern cultures into the ancient Greek and Roman worlds and vice versa. The importance of these outposts for the transmission of culture is represented by the existence of locally made ancient artworks excavated in Iran, Iraq, and Afghanistan that are stylistically related to the Hellenistic art of the Macedonian world of Alexander the Great.

The history of the Silk Road is extremely complex. It cannot be told as a singular chronological narrative. Different cultures and societies rose and vanished along the Silk Road, and peoples migrated from one region to another. In short, for most of its history, there was fluidity as to the dominant cultures along the route or routes. Explaining the rise and fall or disappearance of these cultures involves stopping along the way to consider the chronology of their histories.

Chapter 1 – Rome, Silk, and Ancient Geography

The establishment of the earliest western terminus of the Silk Road has been based on the supposition that Chinese silk was among the major luxuries consumed by wealthy Romans. It has been thought that in the era of the late Roman Republic, which ended in 27 BCE, Chinese silk passed through Parthian merchants to be consumed by Roman patricians. However, it has been convincingly proved that silk available in the Roman markets, lasting well into the imperial period, was woven in western Asia, specifically in Damascus and Mosul. This has been proved by the analysis of the thread; it is distinctly of the type produced by species of silkworms that were raised in western and central Asia.

Many people may not realize that silk is produced in different ways, and since silk was thought to be the most popular item on the Silk Road, it is worth delving into the different ways silk was made. There was also a source for silk in the Indian subcontinent, where the fabric had been produced since around 2500 BCE. Silk produced in India and on the Aegean island of Cos in the 1st century, as well as earlier, was made from cocoons that were naturally vacated by moths. The silk thread was then scraped from the cocoons. In China, however, the method of production of the thread was different. By as early as 4000 BCE, the silk moth was domesticated in China. Here, the cocoons were boiled with the pupae inside. Long strands of silk thread were pulled from the damp cocoons and then woven into fabrics.

The Romans called the producers of silk the people of Seres, a designation derived from the ancient name Serica, which was one of the easternmost countries known to the ancient Greeks and Romans. This does not mean, as early writers on the Silk Road have assumed, what is modern-day China. It merely referred to the origins of silk that was used in Rome. The *Periplus of the Erythrean Sea*, a Greek language maritime guidebook that was written in the 1st century, describes ports on the Red Sea, Africa, the Persian Gulf, and India, as well as mentions lands beyond the known world. "Somewhere on the outer fringe, there is a very great inland city called Thina [or Sinae] from which silk floss, yarn, and cloth are shipped by land...and via the Ganges River." The anonymous author said, "It is not easy to get to this Thina: for rarely do people come from it." This rendering of Thina was based on the information the writer received from Indian traders.

More information on Roman consumption of silk is available in the writings of Pliny the Elder, who lived from 23 to 70 CE. He was confused about the method in which silk was produced. He thought it was made from white down that adhered to leaves. This down, he thought incorrectly, was scraped off to make silk thread. This description is closer to the production of cotton than that of silk. Pliny, in another passage, noted that the silk worn by Roman women was difficult to manufacture and came from a distant land. He objected to it because it allowed "the Roman matron to flaunt transparent raiment in public."

Because it is difficult to identify the source of silk thread, it is not entirely clear where all of the surviving fragments of Roman silk garments originated. The decorative motifs that were woven into the fabric, when they seem to be of Chinese origin, may instead be Indian copies of Chinese designs. The most certain way to prove a fabric found in the West came from China is the presence of Chinese characters woven into the cloth. Textiles unearthed in Palmyra, Syria, are the earliest Chinese fabrics, complete with decorative Chinese characters, that have been found in the West. They date from the 1st to the 3rd centuries CE. More abundant samples of silk fabrics have survived from the Byzantine Empire from the 5th to the 15th centuries. The analysis of around one thousand samples has revealed only a single one that can be identified as Chinese, although there is some evidence that the Byzantines during the reign of Emperor Justinian I, who ruled from 527 to 565 CE, acquired Chinese silk through trade with people of an ancient Iranian culture called the Sogdians.

It was a Byzantine scholar, Cosmas Indicopleustes, who was the first Westerner to write about China. In his *Christian Topography*, dating from about 550 CE, he used the name Tzinista to designate an East Asian country that was called by its inhabitants as Zhōngguó (*zhōng* meaning middle and *guó* meaning state). Later, the Romans used Taugast as the name for China. It was the name commonly used among Turkic peoples of central Asia to designate the country to their east. A historian during the reign of Byzantine Emperor Heraclius (r. 610-641) adopted this name in his writing.

For their part, the Chinese had only unclear ideas of what lay beyond central Asia. There are references to Egypt but not to Rome in the *Weilüe*, a Chinese historical text composed sometime between 239 and 265 CE. In what is known as the *Book of the Later Han*, compiled sometime between 398 and 445 CE, the descriptions of the lands farthest west seem to be those of the Near East, in particular, Iran and Syria. Later Chinese texts from the 8th century again mention the Near East and refer to Constantinople but are silent on any places in greater Europe.

The first encounter between the Chinese and the Romans may have taken place in the early 1st century. It was reported by the 2nd-century historian Florus that during the reign of Augustus (r. 27 BCE-14 CE), among the many delegations from the East were people called Seres. Because this event is not recorded in any other history, it probably did not occur. From Chinese records, it is likely that the envoy Gan Ying was the first to travel west in a mission to the Roman Empire. In 97 CE, he got as far as Mesopotamia, where he intended to sail west. He was advised that the journey was dangerous and long, so he returned to China without seeing the Mediterranean or Rome itself.

If trade had been established in the era of the Roman Empire before the Sack of Rome in 410, one would expect that Roman coins would have turned up in archaeological sites in the East. To date, no ancient Roman coins have been found in China. The earliest Western coins found were all minted in Byzantium dating from the first half of the 6th century CE. It is important to note that along the southwest coast of India, thousands of Roman gold and silver coins have turned up in archaeological excavations. This indicates that significant maritime and overland trade existed between Rome and India. Also, Roman coins have appeared in what is today Vietnam, suggesting that maritime trade between Rome and Southeast Asia predated any land-based commerce between Europe and the Far East.

To summarize, the evidence in the West suggests that it was only sometime after the 1st century CE, at the earliest, that any trade existed between areas in the eastern provinces of the Roman Empire, such as Syria, and the Far East. Clearly, the Romans did not know of the existence of China until much later.

In terms of Western names for the great land of the Far East, the term China was adopted by the English in the 16th century from the Portuguese. Scholars have traced its origin to Persian or possibly Sanskrit. It is more likely derived from the word Qin, the Chinese name of the Qin dynasty, which lasted from 221 to 206 BCE. It was during the Qin dynasty that the various peoples of China were first united under a central government.

Chapter 2 – Han Silk Production and Trade

China's first imperial dynasty, the Qin, was replaced by the Han Dynasty, which rose to power with the Han people dominating in a period of warring ethnic factions contending for power. The first Han emperor, Liu Bang, who reigned from 202 to 195 BCE, succeeded in the pacification of eighteen feudal states, forming a dominion of what consists of part of modern-day China under his rule. He established the capital of the Han Chinese state at Chang'an, modern-day Xi'an. In the early years of the Han dynasty, soldiers were dispatched to the frontiers to protect the empire from barbarian incursions on the frontiers. In order to diminish the frequency of raids by peoples outside Han China, border markets were opened so that those living outside the Han Empire, beyond walled fortifications, could carry out regulated trade with Han merchants. This method of pacification became the Han norm in order to expand influence, as well as to encourage trade. In the wake of organized trade, the Han, through force, could assimilate peoples on the frontier and eventually feed the imperial treasury with income derived from taxation.

The Han policy of establishing regulated trade with peoples beyond the frontiers of their empire required obtaining knowledge of these peoples, of which there were many, what surplus goods they had, and what goods they wished to acquire from the Chinese. The seventh emperor of the Han dynasty, Emperor Wu (r. 141 BCE–87 BCE) in 138 BCE dispatched an envoy named Zhang Qian to form an alliance with nomadic pastoralists called the Yuezhi people who moved into Sogdia in the 2nd century BCE, a loose confederation of indigenous peoples located in what is present-day Kazakhstan, Tajikistan, and Uzbekistan.

Before the arrival of the Yuezhi, the Sogdians had a centuries-old culture that was shaped by their history of conquest by Near Eastern and Mediterranean empires. The Sogdians were ruled first by Persian Cyrus the Great (r. 559 BCE–530 BCE), and then their lands were annexed by Alexander the Great in 328 BCE. The Sogdian confederation of tribes was centered on the city of Samarkand. After the death of Alexander the Great, Sogdia became a part of the Greek Seleucid Empire and then a part of the Greco-Bactrian Kingdom, which extended from northern Iran to the Hindu Kush mountain range and as far as the Oxus River.

The initiation of trade with the Yuezhi was not the only motive for Wu's emissary Zhang Qian's mission. It was his intention to enlist the Yuezhi as Han allies in a battle against the Xiongnu of Mongolia and the Manchurian steppe, which was a menacing threat to the Han Empire on the northern frontier. The Xiongnu was a confederation of nomadic tribes that were united as the Xiongnu Empire under Modu, who ruled from 209 BCE to 174 BCE. Modu's warriors were constantly warring with peoples to the east of the Han Empire and peoples in the west, including the Yuezhi. Like with all movements and aggression by barbarian tribes, the result was the pushing of weaker tribes into new regions. The pressure on these weaker tribes meant that they moved into areas occupied by other tribes and displacing them. This constant tribal migration upset trade and inflicted pressure on settled people like the Han. The wars between the Xiongnu and neighboring peoples continued after Modu's death. As such, it was into an area of unsettled tribal supremacy that Zhang Qian traveled in.

Unfortunately, the diplomat was captured by the Xiongnu in 138 BCE, and they enslaved him for ten years. After escaping, Zhang Qian finally made contact with the Yuezhi, who pastured their livestock to the west of where the Xiongnu were settled. Zhang eventually had to report back to the Han emperor that any alliance with the Yuezhi was not to be, as the Yuezhi showed no interest in fighting against their de facto overlords, the Xiongnu.

Zhang Qian was more successful as an explorer than as a diplomat. His reports of his travels among the peoples of central Asia convinced Han authorities that beyond the frontiers of their empire lay opportunities for the expansion of trade and perhaps tribute through taxation. In his travels, Zhang met the inhabitants of Dayuan, which was an urban center in the Fergana Valley in central Asia that stretched across today's eastern Uzbekistan, southern Kyrgyzstan, and northern Tajikistan. Dayuan was 1,500 kilometers (around 932 miles) from the Han capital of Chang'an. Zhang Qian reported that the residents of Dayuan had Caucasian features, lived in walled cities, were consumers of wine, and raised remarkably hardy horses. Zhang tried unsuccessfully to convince the people of Dayuan to send some of their extraordinary horses to Emperor Wu.

The culture of the people of Dayuan was quite different from the cultures of the nomadic peoples who surrounded them, among which were the Yuezhi. The Fergana Valley had been conquered by Alexander the Great in 329 BCE, where he founded the city of Alexandria Eschate (Alexandria the Furthest) on the banks of the Syr Darya River on the site of the present-day city of Khujand, Tajikistan. Upon the death of Alexander, his walled city fell under the control of the Seleucid Empire and then became a part of the Greco-Bactrian Kingdom. According to the Greek historian Strabo (63 BCE–24 CE), the Greco-Bactrians expanded their kingdom "as far as the Seres [Chinese] and the Phryni," a generic term for the people of the Far

East. There is archaeological evidence of late Hellenistic-inspired statuettes of Greek soldiers that indicates the Greco-Bactrians may have penetrated as far east as modern-day Ürümqi in the Chinese region of Xinjiang.

The Greco-Bactrian Kingdom was founded in 250 BCE when a secessionist Seleucid leader set himself up as King Diodotus I Soter of Bactria. His successor, Diodotus II, was overthrown by the Greek Euthydemus, who, between 210 and 220 BCE, expanded the Greco-Bactrian Kingdom, moving as far east as Xinjiang (modern northwestern China). The Greek historian Strabo wrote that "they [the Greco-Bactrians] extended their empire even as far as the Seres [the Chinese]." The Greco-Bactrians also expanded their sway south under King Demetrius I (r. circa 200 BCE–180 BCE), who successfully annexed modern-day Afghanistan, Pakistan, Punjab, and parts of the Indian subcontinent.

When the diplomat Zhang Qian arrived in Dayuan in about 128 BCE, he saw warriors demonstrate shooting arrows from horseback. This suggests that the residents were, at the time, nomadic herdsmen who had migrated to the city to seek the protection of the Greco-Bactrian Kingdom, which was then being invaded by the Yuezhi. The Yuezhi were being pushed out of their pasture lands by expanding tribes of nomadic pastoralists. The migrating Yuezhi bypassed Dayuan and practiced their nomadic life to the southwest, where they fought off the authority of the declining Greco-Bactrian Kingdom.

On his return east to China, Zhang Qian was again captured by the Xiongnu. He escaped in the midst of a civil war in the Xiongnu Empire and made his way home to Chang'an.

The history of Sogdia, where the Yuezhi eventually "settled," as much as the word can be applied to traditional nomads, is even more complicated. Its geographical location made it susceptible to the force of other migrant tribes following in their footsteps from both the east and the west. In the 1ˢᵗ century CE, Sogdia became the center of a new empire formed by the Yuezhi, who had lived in Bactria. The Kushan Empire extended from Sogdia in the north, through Afghanistan, and into northern India. Kushan Emperor Kanishka the Great (r. circa 127-150 CE), who was probably of Yuezhi ethnicity, reformed and expanded the empire, setting up capitals at Purusapura in the Peshawar Basin (located in modern-day Pakistan and Afghanistan) and Kapisi (near modern-day Bagram, Afghanistan). Kanishka also expanded his empire to the south, taking most of India. By connecting India with central Asia as far north as the Fergana Valley and as far east as Furfan, which was adjacent to the border of Han China, the Kushan Empire was able to efficiently trade north to south and fostered trade from Sogdia to China. It was along these trade routes of the Silk Road that Buddhism made its way from India, where Siddhartha Gautama, its founder, was born about 563 BCE. His teachings slowly spread into central Asia, and the religion reached China in the 2nd century CE, which is when Buddhist monks are first recorded as having translated their texts into Chinese.

Chapter 3 – The Kingdom of Loulan

The first successful concerted effort to expand trading toward the West by the Han emperors themselves began in the 1st century BCE. This mercantile venture was centered on the oasis city of Loulan, where a sophisticated kingdom had grown to dominate the region by the second century BCE.

In Chinese, Turkestan (which included part of modern-day Xinjiang), in what is now a sparsely inhabited wasteland, explorers and archaeologists have discovered a previously unknown ancient culture in what is designated today as the Shanshan Basin. Skirting the southern margins of the Taklamakan Desert, the Shanshan Basin has yielded spectacular archaeological discoveries. In the now desolate region, at the sites of the ancient cities of Niya and Loulan, archaeologists have discovered the remains of a sophisticated culture that had significant importance in connecting central Asia with cultures from the south as far as India.

Archaeological evidence has proved that the people who lived in the urban centers of Niya and Loulan were in regular contact with traders from the south. These southern merchants moved north through the mountain ranges of the Karakoram, Hindu Kush, Pamir,

Kunlun, and Himalayas. Along the route, which passed from the Gandhara region of the Indian subcontinent to the Taklamakan Desert, graffiti carved into stones have been discovered. Some of the stones have images of Siddhartha Gautama, also known as Gautama Buddha, and texts in two Indic scripts, Kharosthi and the later script of Brahmi.

Archaeological evidence from Niya and Loulan paint a complex picture of the cultural origins of the populations of the two cities. Some artifacts have stylistic characteristics that indicate their makers came from the Gandhara region (northwest Pakistan and northeast Afghanistan). Corpses disinterred at Niya and Loulan are not Chinese or Indian; they are instead Caucasoid with fair hair, light skin, and around six feet in height. This leads to speculation that the Niyans and Loulans were descendants of migrants from the Iranian Plateau. The textiles that wrapped these corpses, which date from the 2nd to 4th centuries CE, consist of cotton and silk. The former came from the west and the latter from the east.

Descriptions of the peoples of the region of the Taklamakan Desert exist in two ancient texts, *The History of the Han Dynasty* (82 CE) and the subsequent *History of the Later Han* (445 CE). The region is identified by the Chinese writers as the Kingdom of Shanshan. The two cities in the Kingdom of Shanshan, Niya and Loulan, seem to have vied with each other in importance when it came to the spread of Buddhism and the Indic Kharosthi language.

It was Zhang Qian's report that encouraged Emperor Wu to attack Loulan in 108 BCE. The king of Loulan was captured, and tribute was demanded by the Han emperor. Loulan, through alternating alliances between the Han and the Xiongnu, managed to stave off conquest. In 77 BCE, though, matters came to a head. After a series of Han envoys had been killed by the king of Loulan, Emperor Zhao (r. 87 BCE–74 BCE) sent an envoy named Fu Jiezi to Loulan. He delivered a gift of silk from China to the king of Loulan. The king, delighted with the gift, is said to have become intoxicated, and Fu's guard killed him. According to the Chinese records, Fu's assassin announced, "The Son of Heaven [the Han emperor] has sent me to punish the king, by reason of his crime in turning against Han...Han troops are about to arrive here; do not dare to make any move which would result in yourselves bringing about the destruction of your state." The Chinese then occupied the Kingdom of Loulan and attempted to annex it into the Han Empire under the designation Shanshan. The region, however, in periods when the Chinese showed signs of weakness, either reverted to being an independent kingdom or fell under the control of the Xiongnu. Han records say that in 25 CE, Loulan was allied with the Xiongnu. The Chinese responded by sending an army officer, Ban Chao, to force Loulan to return to Han control. When Ban Chao, along with a small contingent of soldiers, arrived in Loulan, he discovered a Xiongnu delegation negotiating with the king of Loulan. Ban killed the Xiongnu envoys and delivered their heads to King Guang, the ruler of Loulan, who then submitted to Han authority. This ensured that the first leg of the Silk Road from China toward the West was safe for traders and merchants.

Following the pacification of the peoples of the Shanshan Basin and forcing them to accede to Han control, Ban Chao decided to make contact with the far-away Roman Empire. He dispatched an ambassador, Gan Ying, to travel to the West. Exactly what Ban Chao knew about the Romans, whose empire at the time extended to Mesopotamia, is not known. Presumably, he acquired some knowledge of what lay beyond Persia from the traders in Loulan. Ambassador Gan Ying, whose goal was to reach the "western sea," may have reached the Mediterranean or Black Sea. However, it is more likely that he got only as far as the Persian Gulf. Learning that the journey across whatever sea he encountered involved a three-month roundtrip, he abandoned his expedition. His description of the Roman Empire, certainly based on second-hand observations, included information on the goods produced there, among them gold, silver, coins, jade, rhinoceros' horns, coral, amber, glass, and silk rugs with interwoven gold thread. It is clear from Gan Ying's mission that authorities and traders in Loulan believed that commerce and trading with the Han Chinese could be expanded by missions to the unknown West.

It has been suggested that Gan Ying's journey west was sabotaged by the Parthians, whose empire stretched from Mesopotamia, north to the Caspian Sea, and east into central Asia, almost to the frontiers of Chinese Shanshan. The Parthians, wishing to protect their role as the middlemen in the trade between Rome and India, as well as to advance their potential for trade farther east with China, may have discouraged Gan Ying by exaggerating the difficulties of the continuation of his expedition in a long sea crossing to the Roman Empire.

After Gan Ying's journey to the West, the Han emperor worked to cement their control of Shanshan and prevent subsequent kings of Loulan from harboring notions of independence. Soldiers were dispatched to Loulan, where they settled as colonists. By 222 CE, Shanshan had become a formal tributary of the Chinese. Affirmation of the inferior dependent status of Shanshan is indicated by the fact that the king was sent as a hostage to the Chinese court during the reign of the first emperor of the Jin dynasty, Emperor Wu (r. 266-290). The lengths to which the Chinese had to go through to deal with Shanshan indicates that the trade along the Silk Road was financially advantageous to the Han emperor.

In the *History of the Later Han*, which was compiled in the fifth century from earlier texts, it is recorded that the first ambassadors from the Romans arrived in the capital of the Han Empire during the reign of Emperor Huan (r. 146-168). It is not clear whether the emissaries were sent by Antoninus Pius (r. 138-161) or his successor Marcus Aurelius (r. 161-180). The Roman embassy arrived by sea, perhaps via the Gulf of Tonkin, which is located off the coast of northern Vietnam and southern China. This first group of Romans to visit the Han court became suspect because the gifts they presented were objects acquired in Southeast Asia rather than unique objects from Rome itself. It has been surmised by historians that the visitors to the Han court were, in fact, not a group of official ambassadors but rather merchants who had been shipwrecked and had thus lost the Roman goods they intended to deliver to the Chinese. The theory that the first contact between the Romans and the Chinese was through Southeast Asia is confirmed by other texts and archaeological finds involving mercantile connections between Rome and modern-day Cambodia and Vietnam. In 226 CE, a trader named in the texts as Qin Lun—a Chinese version of an unknown Roman name—appeared at the court of Emperor Sun Quan in Nanjing. After describing his Roman homeland, Qin Lun was dispatched back to the West. It is likely that Qin Lun, like earlier merchants, was a Roman trader who landed in Southeast Asia.

Chapter 4 – Buddhists along the Silk Road

The early history of what was to become known in the modern era as the Silk Road does not indicate that the silk trade was the primary goal in forging trade expansion in either the East or the West. The Greeks and Romans were primarily interested in expansion as they pushed into Asia Minor, and the Han Chinese were motivated to expand west in their goal of trading foodstuffs, horses, and a limited range of luxury goods with the settled and semi-nomadic peoples living there.

The towns and cities along the ancient trading routes, some of which were merely small oases and others sophisticated urban centers, were important not only for the exchange of goods but for the transmission of culture in all its forms, including language and religion.

In order to understand the spread of culture via the Silk Road, it is necessary to turn to the prosperous oasis city of Kucha. It was the gateway to the Chinese trade route that skirted the Taklamakan Desert to the north. Like Loulan, it became the nexus for the transmission of culture. The language of Kucha, Kuchean, came from the same Indo-European language group as Sanskrit, the original language for the expression of Buddhist teachings.

The Chinese first interacted with the peoples of Kucha in the late second century BCE. Han Emperor Wu sent his general Li Guangli to visit the kingdom of Fergana in modern-day Uzbekistan. On the way, he visited Kucha. Like in Loulan, the leaders of Kucha had attempted to appease the Xiongnu confederation, but as the Xiongnu weakened, the Kuchans became allied with the Han Chinese. In 65 BCE, the king of Kucha traveled to Chang'an, and after that, the Chinese had an official report on the oasis settlements along the northern route of the Silk Road around the Taklamakan Desert. The reports sent back by the officials in Kucha became incorporated into the official history of the Han dynasty.

The extent of the presence of the Hans in the region is difficult to assess. The oasis kingdoms along the northern route of what we call the Silk Road were continuously at war with one another. Thus, Kucha, in 46 BCE, was defeated by the neighboring oasis kingdom of Yarkand. The Han Chinese seem to have subsequently exerted control intermittently over various oases surrounding Kucha. General Ban Chao, who was named governor of the region in 91 CE, gained formal control of Kucha itself. His garrison at Kucha, which he placed under the control of the Bai family, lasted less than twenty years. Peoples of the region rose up against the Chinese rule and destroyed the Chinese garrison at Kucha. The Bai family, from time to time, succeeded over the centuries in gaining dominance over one oasis or another. They became Buddhists, and Buddhism became the dominant religion in Kucha by the 4th century.

It was in Kucha that Buddhist writings were translated from Sanskrit into Chinese by Kumarajiva (lived 344 to 413 CE). Kumarajiva was the son of a devout Buddhist mother who abandoned her husband and settled in a Buddhist nunnery. She traveled with her son to Gandhara, where Kumarajiva studied Hinayana Buddhism and then studied under a Mahayana Buddhist monk. He returned home to Kucha, bringing the two strands of Buddhism back to his people.

In 384 CE, the city of Kucha was conquered again, this time by the Chinese general Lü Chuang. Kucha was said to have had thousands of pagodas and temples, and the palace of the Bai kings was described as being equal to the residence of the gods. The holy Kumarajiva was kidnapped around 390 BCE, and according to his biography, he fathered children, which was against his Buddhist vows. Eventually, he arrived in the Chinese capital of the Jin dynasty (265–420 CE), Chang'an, in 401, where he was put in charge of translating Buddhist texts. Among the many texts he translated was the Lotus Sutra (a sutra is the Sanskrit word for a work said to be by Buddha himself). Kumarajiva's texts were widely circulated, and understanding them was eased by the Chinese invention of the pinyin system, in which certain characters were developed to represent syllables of foreign words. The expansion of the Chinese language so that certain Sanskrit words for Buddhist concepts could be understood may have involved the invention of as many as 35,000 new Chinese words.

The translation of Sanskrit texts in this period was not restricted to the Jin capital, Chang'an. In Kucha and elsewhere along the Silk Road, Buddhist texts were translated into local languages.

During the lifetime of Kumarajiva, work began on the now world-famous caves of Kizil, which are located 67 kilometers (almost 42 miles) west of Kucha. Discovered by a German explorer in 1909, the 339 excavated caves were decorated with paintings that have been used by art historians to unravel the cultural history of the region. The caves of Kizil consist of single rooms centered on a pillar, or stupa, around which Buddhists walked, expressing their devotion to Buddha. The construction of the caves is similar to those in India at Ajanta, near Bombay, and other early Buddhist caves in India. Some of the paintings, such as that of cave 38, show Indian gods and flaming Buddhas depicted in a distinctly Indian style. They were painted by artists from India or copied from drawings brought from India. Other caves are decorated with illustrations of Jataka tales, which are stories concerning Gautama Buddha's previous incarnations as both humans and animals. The tales, dating from 300 BCE to 400 CE, involved Buddha helping characters who found themselves in trouble. Since the discovery of the caves of Kizil, antiquarians from several nations have removed a lot of the artwork and deposited it in museums in the West.

The Bai family continued to rule in Kucha from the 6th through the 8th centuries. During this period, taxes were rendered to the reigning Chinese dynasties. Information on trade has been gleaned from Kuchan official passes for caravans that exist for the period of 641 to 644. Generally, the caravans were small, with less than ten men and a small number of animals, either donkeys or horses. Since the roads were safe, the caravans could consist of a small number of men who didn't require the protection of warriors. In 648, Tang Chinese (618-907) soldiers conquered Kucha again, wresting it from being a dependency of the Western Turkic Khaganate, which was formed at the beginning of the 7th century. Tang Chinese control over Kucha, the easternmost city along the northern Silk Road, was intermittently broken by revolts and incursions by Tibetans and Sogdians. The Tang Anxi Protectorate (647-784), established by the Tang military government, managed to hold onto control of Kucha, but contact with Chang'an along the Silk Road was occasionally broken. A Chinese general named Guo Xin held control of Kucha from 766. He ruled in isolation until 790 when the Tibetans from the south moved in. They, in turn, were displaced by the Uyghurs, who controlled the area from the early 9th century to the rise of the Mongol Empire in the 13th century.

Trade between China and the Kuchans throughout the 7th and 13th centuries was mainly restricted to horses. These were obtained from the nomadic tribes who grazed their herds north of Kucha and from the Sogdians to the west. The horses were exchanged for agricultural goods, steel, or cloth. There is also evidence that there was a monetized economy in the form of Chinese coins. When the Tang withdrew from Kucha in 755, a local currency was minted.

Chapter 5 – Turfan: An Oasis on the Silk Road

The second-most important oasis city on the Silk Road route to the north of the Taklamakan Desert was Turfan. The original inhabitants of the Turfan region were called Chü-shih by the Chinese, meaning people who lived in felt tents. By 60 BCE, the Han had pushed out the Xiongnu, a loose confederacy of nomadic tribes who lived in the eastern Eurasian Steppe, and controlled the land once occupied by the Chü-shih. The Han, for administrative purposes, split the newly subservient peoples into eight states, making the region around Turfan, the former Chü-shih kingdom, their center of operations. The garrison at Turfan included a military colony, and by 273 CE, the majority of the population of Turfan was primarily Chinese immigrants. The city changed hands regularly, but for the most part, it remained under Chinese control. With the collapse of the Western Qin dynasty in the 4th century CE, Turfan suffered from incursions by nomadic tribesmen. It was, after a concerted military effort, that the region around Turfan was restored to Chinese control under the Ch'ü family, who administered the territory from their capital at Kao-ch'ang some 40 kilometers (almost 25 miles) from modern-day Turfan.

Kao-ch'ang served as the administrative capital of the Turfan region under members of the Ch'ü family, who styled themselves as the kings of Liang. It was under Chü-ch'ü An-chou that an important Buddhist monastery was founded near Turfan. When it was explored by European archaeologists in the early 20th century, it revealed a treasure trove of information about the cultural history of the Turfan segment of the Silk Road.

In 460 CE, Chü-ch'ü An-chou was overthrown by a confederacy of nomadic tribes from the Gobi Desert, who then set up their own kingdom in Kao-ch'ang. In spite of the barbarian incursions, Turfan remained the base for administration under the Ch'ü family of kings (500–640) and subsequently under the Chinese administrators of the Tang dynasty (618–907) and finally the Uyghur Qocho kingdom (866–1283). By 981, there were more than fifty Buddhist temples in the vicinity of Turfan.

When the southern route around the Taklamakan Desert fell into disuse after 500 CE, travelers chose the northern route that passed through the city of Turfan. A description of the city exists in the writings of a Chinese monk named Xuanzang (c.602–664), who set out from Chang'an for India in 629. His purpose was to study Sanskrit Buddhist texts. From the westernmost city that was under the control of the Tang Chinese, Xuanzang proceeded west across the Gobi Desert and arrived in Turfan, which was about 650 kilometers (almost 404 miles) northeast of Kucha, in 630.

From Turfan, the Silk Road passed into Sogdia. After its invasion by the Muslims in the 8th century, the dominant religion, after a period of gradual conversion, became Islam.

Sogdia was a network of city-states where merchants traveled from one oasis to another, linking with Byzantium, India, Indochina, and China. Since its exploration by Zhang Qian during the reign of Han Emperor Wu in the 2nd century BCE, Sogdia was known to the Chinese as Kangju. Trade along the Silk Road between Sogdia and China, which had proceeded more or less unhindered in the Tang era, was interrupted by the collapse of the Tang Dynasty in 907 CE.

In the north and west of China, the Uyghur tribal confederacy broke up in the mid-10th century. The Uyghurs, a Turkic ethnic group that migrated from Mongolia into the region north of the Taklamakan Desert in the 9th century, converted to Islam in the 10th century. With multi-ethnic conflicts rife along the north and south Silk Road routes around the Taklamakan Desert, there was an interruption in long-distance trade.

Although these kinds of disturbances along the Silk Road interrupted trade, the rise of a people called the Khitans might have interrupted it worse. The Khitans were a nomadic people who moved with the seasons over grazing lands in modern-day Mongolia, Russian Far East, and parts of China. They were, according to scholars, proto-Mongolians who spoke Khitan.

A leader of the Yila tribe of the Khitans, by the name of Abaoji, set out in the first quarter of the 10th century to unify the Khitans and conquer neighboring peoples. Leading a 70, 000-man cavalry, he rode into Shanxi (a modern-day province of northern China), where he made an alliance with the military governor, Li Keyong, who in 833 had unified and pacified Shanxi under the authority of the Tang Dynasty. From the capital of Chang'an, the emperors of the Tang Dynasty created a highly cultured civilization—according to some, it was the golden age of China—and through force, they pacified nomadic tribes to the west along the Silk Road. These tribes of Inner Asia were put under a protectorate system and required to pay tribute to China.

With his successes in taking Tang Chinese territories in northern China, Abaoji assumed the title of Khagan of the Khitans. Later known after his death as Emperor Taizu of Liao (r. 916-926), he attempted to organize his people under an administration that combined the traditions of nomadic society and the Chinese system of government that had been adopted by the sedentary peoples he annexed into his empire. For instance, in Abaoji's court, Chinese formalities were observed. He went so far as to call himself Celestial Emperor in the Chinese style. In contradiction to Khitan tradition, in which leadership was won by merit, he named his son as the heir apparent. By the time of his death, Abaoji had conquered all of the tribes to the east in the Korean Peninsula, the Russian Far East, and Manchuria. Also, he had spread his authority well into the Mongolian Plateau. However, Abaoji did not live to follow his ambition to move south to attack the Tang Chinese. After an internecine struggle, Taizong became the second emperor of Liao (r. 927-947). He succeeded where his father had failed—he marched into China, proceeded to cross the Yellow River, and threatened to move west to Chang'an. Rebellions and treachery among his own forces and the Chinese rebel families he conquered forced Taizong to retreat and return beyond the Yellow River. When he died, his successor could not keep the territorial gains. The Liao dynasty faded in importance until it fell to the Northern Song dynasty of China in 1125.

Further disruptions in the trade along the Silk Road were caused by warfare in the north between the Song Chinese and the rival Great Jin dynasty (1115-1234). The conflict forced the Song armies and court to retreat to the south, giving up control of a vast swath of northern China, principally Manchuria, to the Jurchen rebels, who were at first allies of the Jin and later became their overlords.

Following their retreat to the south, trade for the Song Chinese came to be less reliant on the Silk Road, as it had become increasingly dangerous and unreliable. Commerce along the Silk Road was, in part, supplanted by maritime trade with Japan, Southeast Asia, and around the Indian Ocean. Chinese ports along the southern coast, such as Guangzhou and Quanzhou, became important trading centers with Arab, Persian, Malay, and Tamil traders who carried out their business there.

Chapter 6 – The Legend of Prester John

In the early Middle Ages, Europeans had only the sketchiest of ideas of what laid east beyond Mesopotamia. Legends of Alexander's conquests in the East were passed down in oral literature and eventually put into writing. These were, for the most part, fanciful tales that referred to strange creatures such as Amazons, Cynocephali (dog-headed men), Sciopods (one-legged men who were swift runners), and Anthropophagi (men with faces on their chests). Strange beasts were also said to inhabit the East, like unicorns and serpents with two feet.

European interest in the lands that lay in the East beyond the Mediterranean was stimulated by the fervor for crusading against the Muslims. The Muslims had expanded their sphere of influence well beyond the Holy Land when the First Crusade was launched in 1096. The initiation of trade with the unknown Eastern lands was of less importance than spreading the Christian religion to counter Muslim expansionism in the East.

In the 12th century, the legends of the East were expanded with the inclusion of the tale of Prester John. In 1122, a man claiming to be the patriarch of India arrived in Rome, demanding papal confirmation of his office. Contemporary texts exist which purported to record Prester John's description of India as he presented it to Pope Callixtus II. Prester John, it was said, told the pope that he lived in the huge city of Hulna, which was inhabited by devout Christians and surrounded by twelve monasteries. The tale of a vibrant Christian community beyond the Tigris River was reiterated by the German chronicler Bishop Otto of Freising. He wrote in 1145 that he had heard from a Syrian bishop that a king and priest named John ruled over a vast kingdom of Nestorian Christians descended from the Magi, which many readers may be familiar with their depiction in the story of the birth of Jesus as the three men who traveled from the East to pay homage to the infant Christ. Otto of Freising reported that the eastern king John would have come to the aid of the besieged Christian Crusaders in the Near East had he not been prevented from doing so by the impossibility of ferrying his army across the Tigris.

The legend of Prester John was further expanded in an anonymously authored *Letter of Prester John*, which was created sometime before 1180 and addressed to Byzantine Emperor Manuel I Comnenus (r. 1143-1180). The letter became a very popular document, and there are more than 120 manuscript copies of it.

In the letter, Prester John says that he wishes to travel to the West and visit the Sepulcher of Christ. He says that he rules over a vast kingdom with 62 Christian sub-kings and that his realm is extraordinarily prosperous, flowing with milk and honey. It is adjacent to Paradise, has a fountain of youth, and there is no venial sin in his land. Prester John reports that he has an enormous army with knights and crossbowmen. In summary, he concludes, "There is no king as powerful in this world as am I."

The manuscript copies of the letter varied, and the description of Prester John's kingdom was expanded. For instance, in the copies created in England, it was said that in the eastern court of Prester John, there were some 11,000 Englishmen. In France, the copies of the letter claimed that Prester John had 11,000 French knights in his command.

The popularity of the *Letter of Prester John* suggests that there was a widespread hope in Europe during the Middle Ages that a powerful Christian community in the East could assist in the Crusaders' struggle against the Muslim "infidels." Besides that, the fact that there was a spectacular kingdom somewhere in the uncharted territory of the East supplied a kind of hope for a better world among the Europeans.

The Arab geographers in the courts of the Muslim enemies of the Crusaders had equally fanciful notions about what lay to the east of their expanding caliphates. From tales related by seaborne traders who penetrated the East, Muslim scholars concocted confusing reports of India, the East Indies, and China. By the early 14th century, a Kurdish geographer named Abu al-Fida (1273-1331) stated that knowledge of China was "as good as unknown to us; there being few travellers who arrive from these parts, such as might furnish us with intelligence." What little information that was conveyed in the Arab geographical texts relating to the East was not adopted by the Europeans, who, for some reason, ignored the Arab geographical texts, despite having an enthusiastic interest in the scientific writings of the Muslims.

The Europeans were knowledgeable about Christians in the far reaches of the Levant, though. They were adherents to a doctrine condemned by the Christians of the Eastern Rite in Constantinople and the Roman Catholic Church. The Nestorians held the heretical view that in Christ there was but one person with two natures, divine and human. The head of the Nestorian Church was in Baghdad, and their churches were spread throughout the Near East from Syria to Persia. The Nestorians were active proselytizers, and by the 8th century, Nestorian churches could be found in Turkestan, China, and among the nomadic tribes in Mongolia.

The Nestorian Christians came into contact with the Chinese in the 12th century. A breakaway Chinese king, Yelü Dashi, led a group of nomadic Khitan clans into central Asia, where he set himself up as the emperor of Qara Khitai, also known as Western Liao. He established a central authority over a vast region encompassing trade routes around Lake Balkhash. He set up his capital at Balasagun in modern-day Kyrgyzstan. To the west of Qara Khitai, in what is now Iran and Iraq, the Seljuk Sultanate held sway. The enormous armies of Yelü Dashi and the Seljuks met on the battlefield at Qatwan, located north of Samarkand in modern-day Uzbekistan, in 1141. Yelü Dashi's forces prevailed, and he moved on to Samarkand, where he accepted the allegiance of the Muslim leaders there and established a tribute state. It was Yelü Dashi's tolerance of Nestorian Christians in his empire that no doubt became the basis for the legend of Prester John, which proliferated in Europe after the First Crusade (1095–1099).

Chapter 7 – Genghis Khan, Ruler of the Whole World

In the 10th century, the proto-Mongol tribes living in the region of the upper reaches of the Amur River began to leave their ancestral lands in what is today Inner Mongolia and Manchuria. They moved south and west, invading the northern reaches of China, where they founded the Liao dynasty (916-1125). Under the name of the Qara Khitai, they established themselves as sedentary farmers, established a capital city named Huangdu (later Shangjing), and adopted a system of hereditary leadership, abandoning their traditional tribal system of electing a leader. Situated along the Silk Road, the peoples of the Khitan federation had ready access to the ununified states of China. It was along the Silk Road that elements of Chinese culture traveled, such as the idea that stabilization of taxes was advantageous to the growth of wealth. Around 920, the first ruler of the Liao dynasty, Abaoji (r. 916-926), adopted the Chinese name of Taizu. With a need for written documents to facilitate the administration of the Khitan people, the Liao emperor had his court scholars adapt a script from written documents that came into the empire from Chinese traders along the Silk Road. With the knowledge of Chinese culture that traveled north with traders, the Liao emperors were inspired to invade the richer and more sophisticated Chinese.

In 960, fifty years after the collapse of the Tang dynasty in China, the country was unified under the Song dynasty (969-1279). The Song ruled a much smaller swath of China than the Tang. The third Song emperor, Zhenzong (r. 968-1022), negotiated a treaty with Liao to the north, promising to annually deliver a tribute of 200,000 bolts of silk as well as a vast amount of silver. This treasure passed along one of the routes of the Silk Road, as did other goods in the period of peace between the Liao and the Song. Paying a tribute in silk was traditional with the Chinese, and it became a means of exchange that was ubiquitous on the Silk Road in regions adjacent to China. The bolts of silk turned over to the Liao could be used as payment for foodstuffs and horses raised by sedentary farmers and nomadic herdsmen. In turn, the merchants outside and within Liao territory could use the bolts of silk as currency to acquire other goods they required.

There was a gradual coalescing of nomadic Mongol tribes north of the Liao lands, who also assimilated with other tribes who ranged over the central Asian steppes. In 1155, a boy named Temüjin was born into a Mongol clan. He acquired unusual abilities as a warrior, and Temüjin eventually acquired control of all of Mongolia. His demonstrated ability as a warrior and a statesman placed him in good stead when a *kurultai*, or Mongol political and military council, met in 1206 to consider his worthiness as a leader. Temüjin, better known as Genghis Khan, was appointed as the great khan of the Mongols. From this point on, he extended his power to form the greatest empire the world had ever seen. The many cultures that came to be dominated by the Mongols delivered tribute and traded amongst themselves using the Silk Road. With Mongol control, the trade routes became safer, and traveling with merchandise from west to east and vice versa became less complicated when the Mongols instituted common regulations for passes to travel along segments of the Silk Road.

Genghis Khan subdued the forest people to the north in Siberia, and he attacked the people of the Gobi Desert, then forming a full third of China. He also conquered the Karluks, a confederacy of nomadic Turkic peoples west of the Altai Mountains in central Asia, and subdued the closely allied Muslim Uyghurs, who occupied several oases across the Taklamakan Desert, thus controlling the Silk Road. He took the Khitans into his empire and then set out to conquer China itself. In March of 1211, Genghis Khan declared war on the remnants of the Jin in northern China, which was then under the control of the Jurchens. The going was slow, taking up to two years, during which Genghis Khan took the opportunity to conquer the Jurchens in Manchuria. In 1215, he took Beijing. He immediately returned to Mongolia and dealt with a rebellion in Qara Khitai, where he was received with enthusiasm by Muslims who believed themselves to be oppressed by the Buddhists.

By this time, the Mongols were in control of all of central Asia up to the river Syr Darya, which formed the border with Iran. With respect to the Silk Road, this Mongol suzerainty was an important impetus to the increase in traffic and trade. Iran, then under the control of Ala ad-Din Muhammad II (r. 1200–1220), the shah of the Khwarezmian dynasty, was attacked by Genghis Khan, who led between 150,000 and 200,000 soldiers as he marched toward the west. In September of 1219, Genghis crossed the Syr Darya and penetrated Khwarezmia as far as Bukhara (in modern-day Uzbekistan), then chased down Ala ad-Din Muhammad as he fled south into Bactra (present-day Balkh) and then to Nishapur and Rey (present-day Tehran). Genghis Khan leveled the country and killed many inhabitants; however, he spared the artisans and the Muslim clergy. The latter escaped retribution because Genghis Khan had a policy of protecting all religions and permitting all religious practices within his empire. The son of Ala ad-Din Muhammad, Jalal ad-Din Mingburnu (r. 1220–1231), kept up with the war, retreating into Sogdiana (present-day states of Samarkand and Bokhara in Uzbekistan, Sughd in Tajikistan, and parts of Afghanistan). Genghis

Khan's army pursued his enemy into Sogdiana, where his soldiers carried out ethnic cleansing on a grand scale. Jalal was forced to retreat across the Indus River, where he attempted to rebuild the Khwarezmian Empire. Genghis Khan did not immediately press on in pursuit of Jalal, but in 1222, he besieged Multan (in modern-day Pakistan). The Mongols were forced to withdraw, though, on account of the heat, and Genghis Khan then returned to the seat of his empire in Mongolia.

Due to the conquests in the west by Genghis Khan, the complex and inconsistent trading regulations and the interruption of trade due to local conflicts were slowly ameliorated. With the Mongols in charge, traders could move greater distances before off-loading their goods and handing them over to traders familiar with the local routes of the Silk Road. With the rise of the Mongols, trade along the routes of the Silk Road expanded, both in distance traveled as well as in the volume of goods moved. As the Mongol Empire expanded, so did the length of some of the routes of the Silk Road.

Rather than taking the most direct route home, Genghis Khan's army crossed the Caucasus Mountains, where they encountered the Georgians. The Georgians set up defensive positions in Ukraine, which was then under the control of the Kipchak Turks. The Russians were summoned to help in the battle against the Mongols but were roundly defeated on May 31st, 1222, by allies of Genghis Khan. Mongol Georgia was to become an important starting point for European traders to connect with the northern route along the silk road.

By 1222, the elderly Genghis Khan was facing his own mortality. He had heard that Chinese Taoists were in possession of a secret remedy against death, and so, he summoned a Taoist master to his traveling court, who told him that there were remedies to prolong life but not to avoid death. He advised temperance and good living. The Great Khan listened and then set out for Mongolia, arriving in 1225. Although weary of war, Genghis Khan personally led his army across the Gobi Desert and attacked the Tangut people in northwest China.

It was during this time that Genghis Khan pushed to attack the people of the Western Xia, which are now known as the Chinese provinces of Ningxia, Gansu, Qinghai, Shaanxi, Xinjiang, and parts of Inner and Outer Mongolia. However, it would be his last season of fighting, as Genghis Khan died in 1227 before the Tanguts capitulated. However, the Western Xia, where the Silk Road ran from northern China to central Asia, finally fell under the control of the Mongols. With the Mongols dominating such a large area, encompassing China to the doorstep of Europe in Georgia and Ukraine, trading along the Silk Road became safe and profitable once again.

Because a successor to Genghis Khan could only be elected from his bloodline by a *kurultai*, the assembling of potential candidates took time since they had to be summoned from the far reaches of the Mongol Empire. Finally, Ögedei, Genghis's third son, was appointed as the next great khan, ruling from 1229 to 1241. Among his courtiers were warriors from his family who distinguished themselves with strings of victories that greatly expanded the empire as well as trade. Korea was conquered in 1236, thus pushing the Silk Road farther east. Ögedei Khan's successors as great khan annexed Tibet around 1250. This resulted in an increased movement of goods and ideas from Tibet, which moved along a Silk Road route that went north and east into China.

The Mongols renewed attacks on the Song Chinese emperors, who managed to hold off the Mongol armies from 1234 to 1279. In the west in 1236, the Mongols under the leadership of Ögedei Khan forced the Christian Georgians to become vassals of the Mongol state. This allowed for the extension of a safe Silk Road route up to the frontier with Christian Europe. The Armenians had also fallen under the sway of the Mongols as allies in their struggle to resist the imposition of Islam on their state. In 1254, Hethum I, the king of Armenia (r. 1226-1270), submitted his kingdom to Mongol suzerainty. To confirm this, he sent his brother Sempad to Karakorum in 1247, which was the Mongol capital from 1235 to 1260. (Karakorum was in what today is the Övörkhangai Province of

Mongolia near the modern town of Kharkhorin.) Sempad did not travel east along the Silk Road but rather went by sea to the court of the Mongol Empire. The arrangement between Armenia and Ögedei Khan was ratified in 1254 when King Hethum traveled overland across Asia along the Silk Road to meet the great khan. His trip was recorded in a text, *The Journey of Haithon, King of Little Armenia, To Mongolia and Back*, by the Armenian court historian Kirakos Gandzaketsi (c. 1200-1271). The story of the journey became popular in Europe and Russia, where there was a great interest in the Mongol Empire, the court of the great khan, and the trade along the overland routes from the exotic Eastern cultures. Among those most particularly drawn to the account were traders and merchants, who looked to get as much information on the Silk Road before engaging in what they believed would be profitable ventures to the seat of power of the mighty Mongol Empire.

The northwestern region of the Mongol Empire split from the control of the Mongol court in Karakorum in 1259. It became a separate khanate known as the Kipchak Khanate or the Ulus of Jochi. The latter name was applied because the region of the Mongol Empire, including southern Russia and Kazakhstan, had been given by Genghis Khan to his eldest son Jochi. When Jochi died, the area came under the control of his son, Batu Khan. In 1235, Batu led his army westward, capturing Volga Bulgaria, a state at the confluence of the Volga and Kama Rivers, in 1236 and part of the Ukrainian steppe in 1237. The Crimean Peninsula was conquered by the Mongols in 1238. Batu then moved north into Kievan Rus' and invaded Poland and Hungary and laid siege to Vienna.

As he realized he was facing a stronger foe, Batu retreated from Vienna. While doing so, he placed Bulgaria under Mongol control. It was under the reign of Batu Khan (r. 1227-1255) that the Mongol Empire, which was at the doorstep of Europe and Russia, became known as the Golden Horde. This name first appeared in Russian texts dating from the middle of the 16th century; however, the origins of the designation remain shrouded in mystery. It is suspected that the word "horde" was derived from the Mongolic word *ordu*, meaning camp or headquarters. The appellation "golden" may have been derived from the golden tent used by Batu Khan.

With the Mongol Empire so close to the heart of European commerce, it is understandable that merchants in the newly rising city-states of Italy, as well as the various dukedoms and kingdoms in other regions of Europe, would begin to cast their eyes to the East in search of profits. This expansion of trade with the East along the continually lengthening Silk Road was even used by the Catholic Church, as clerics piggybacked on trading missions as a means of increasing papal authority through missionary work.

The imminent danger to Europe posed by the Golden Horde and indeed all of the Mongols, who were known collectively as the Tartars in the West, was remarked upon by Pope Alexander IV (pontiff from 1254 to 1261). His proclamation to what was referred to as "civilized nations" was intended to raise awareness of the threat from the East. He wrote, "There rings in the ears of all...a terrible trumpet of dire forewarning which...[of] the scourge of Heaven's wrath in the hands of the inhuman Tartars, erupting as it were from the secret confines of Hell." This kind of scaremongering had little effect on Christian merchants driven by cupidity rather than religious purity.

The expansion of the Golden Horde by Batu Khan, in effect, paved the way for Europeans to travel the full extent of the Silk Road through territories under the control of a single authority. The Mongol Empire, which extended from Europe to China, facilitated travel and trade through an assortment of minor kingdoms and cultures that, in the past, had hindered free passage for commerce. All of the different tribal, ethnic, and political entities along the Silk Road, which were now under tight Mongol control, offered safe passage for travelers and merchants.

In Europe, the rise of the Mongols, or Tartars as they were known there, was noted by church leaders. A Dominican friar from Hungary on a journey into Mongol-held Russia in 1235 reported that the Mongols were about to conquer Rome and thus claim world domination and consequently destroy the Christian Church. According to Europeans at the time, the Mongols were beasts of the vilest character who were bent on a number of plots to upset the Near East and Europe itself. Pope Gregory IX (pontiff from 1227 to 1241) tried and failed to organize a Crusade against the Mongols. In March 1245, Pope Innocent IV (pontiff from 1243 to 1254) wrote letters to the "King and peoples of the Tartars," explaining Christian doctrine and asking for an explanation of the Mongol attacks against Christian peoples. These were to be presented by two groups of friars. One party was to travel to the Near East along the Silk Road to seek out the leaders of the Mongol forces, while another party was to travel through Poland and Russia to deliver the messages to the leader of the Mongols in Asia.

After passing through the Holy Land, the Dominican Friar, André de Longjumeau, arrived at Tabriz (in northwestern Iran). He delivered the pope's missives to Baycu Noyan, the leader of the Mongol forces in Armenia and Persia. Along the northern route to the Mongol headquarters, the Dominican Ascelin of Cremona, as the head of the papal delegation, traveled to Baycu's summer camp in the Armenian highlands in 1245. There he had the pope's letters translated into Persian and ensured that they were sent off to the court of the great khan at Karakorum in central Asia.

A third embassy was also sent to the Mongols. This one was led by the Franciscan friar Giovanni da Pian del Carpine. Setting out from Lyon in 1245, the ambassadors were joined by a Polish Franciscan, Brother Benedict, who would be able to act as a translator when the group passed through Slavic-speaking lands. They met Batu Khan and delivered letters from the pope. He convinced them that they needed to proceed to the court of the new great khan, Güyük (r. 1246–1248), who was the grandson of Genghis Khan. Their journey along the Silk Road took them through the former Khwarezmian Empire, where they saw "many devastated cities, destroyed castles, deserted villages," and through Qara Khitai, where they suffered from the intense cold. They eventually reached Güyük's camp near Karakorum in 1246.

At the camp, the Franciscans witnessed the ceremonies surrounding the enthronement of Güyük, the new great khan. Friar Giovanni da Pian del Carpine recorded that it was his observation that the great khan was a very intelligent man. He also noted that the Christians (Nestorians) who served in his household were of the belief that he would soon convert to Christianity. In spite of this, Güyük's reply to Pope Innocent IV was an uncompromising rebuttal of the pope's position. Güyük wrote that he rejected the pope's demand that the Mongols become Christian and assent to the superior power of the papacy.

> How dost thou know whom God forgives, to whom he shows mercy? By the power of God from the going up of the sun to his going down He had delivered all the lands to Us...Now you say with a sincere heart: 'We shall become your subject...' Thou in person, at the head of the kings, must all together at once come to do homage to Us. We shall then recognize your submission.

The pope's embassy returned along the Silk Road via Kiev, which they reached on June 9th, 1247. Over the course of their journey, Friar Giovanni and his party had covered some 6,000 kilometers (around 3,730 miles). While the envoys of Pope Innocent IV may have been unsuccessful in convincing the great khan of the supremacy of the Christian Church in Rome, Friar Giovanni, in his account of his journey, *Ystoria Mongalorum*, wrote very useful descriptions of the lands his mission passed through. The *Ystoria Mongalorum* is the first European chronicle of Mongol history, and it was chronicles like this that helped to motivate European traders to seek the fortunes offered by commerce with the East.

The introduction to Giovanni's text reveals what became, for Europeans, the beginnings of knowledge about the Mongols, who were posing a severe threat to the Christian world. Giovanni wrote, "Wishing to write an account of the Tartars in which readers will be able to find their way about, we will divide it into chapters." These chapters deal with descriptions of the country of the Mongols and the peoples and religions of the Mongol Empire. In the final chapter, Giovanni discussed "how war should be waged against them." The detail of Giovanni's account is significant. Under the rubric of Mongol methods of warfare, he describes the organization of their army, weapons, armor, and siege tactics. His anthropological observations included, among other things, marriage customs, food, clothes, and burial practices. With respect to the geography of the Mongol Empire, Giovanni only discusses what he observed on his journey to and from Karakorum. The information Giovanni had gleaned on his trip was circulated through lectures he gave to his fellow Franciscans.

The next recorded contact between the Mongols and the Europeans occurred in December 1248 when two Nestorian Christians from within the Mongol Empire arrived in Cyprus, where King Louis IX of France (r. 1226-1270) was preparing for his Crusade against the Muslims in Egypt. The emissaries falsely said that the Mongol general Eljihidey, who commanded troops in Persia, and the Great Khan Güyük had converted to Christianity. The ambassadors also claimed that Güyük's mother was the daughter of Prester John, someone the Europeans knew well from popular legends. All of this was good news for the Crusaders under King Louis, and they sought to affirm the assistance of the Mongols in their fight against the Muslims. André de Longjumeau, already having made contact with the Mongols, was dispatched to Tabriz with appropriate gifts, but on his arrival, he learned that the Great Khan Güyük had died. The Mongol general Eljihidey sent the ambassadors to Karakorum, where the regent, Sorghaghtani Beki, in the midst of arranging for her son to ascend to the Mongol imperial throne, understood the gifts offered by the ambassadors to be a symbol of France's and Latin Europe's submission to the soon-to-be great khan. Sorghaghtani Beki then sent a letter to Louis IX, demanding that he appear at her court and deliver up appropriate tribute.

However, Louis, preoccupied with other matters, abandoned his attempted alliance with the Mongols. A Franciscan in his entourage, William of Rubruck, convinced the French king to permit him to travel as a missionary to see Batu and convince him that the Mongols of the Golden Horde should convert to Christianity. William and a companion, Friar Bartolomeo of Cremona, set off from Cyprus in May of 1253. They passed through Constantinople and sailed across the Black Sea to the Crimean Peninsula. They then rode on horseback, accompanied by a wagon train, to the camp of Sartaq Khan, the son and eventual successor to Batu Khan. Sartaq sent them on to Batu's camp beyond the Volga, and Batu, in turn, sent the friars on to the court of the new Great Khan Möngke (r. 1251-1259) at Karakorum. There, they were allowed to stay for six months. However, William of Rubruck and his companion were unsuccessful in their missionary goals.

In his account of the Mongols, William of Rubruck describes many details of life in the capital, mentioning the use of Chinese paper money, the scribes who wrote in Chinese characters, and the appearance and practices of Buddhist monks. William also notes the presence of Europeans in the Mongol capital, among whom was a Parisian goldsmith who had made a silver tree and four silver lions for the palace of the great khan. According to William, there were twelve pagan temples, two mosques, and a Nestorian church in the capital, the latter which was used by the Hungarians, Russians, Georgians, and Armenians in the community, as well as some of the khan's own family. William was unsuccessful in reaching his goal, the conversion of the great khan. He reported that the Great Khan Möngke had told William of his belief in the last conversation they had together. "As God has given different fingers to the hand, so he has given different ways to men." William left behind his companion Friar Bartolomeo and departed Karakorum with little to show for his missionary zeal. He arrived at Batu's camp in 1254, crossed the Caucasus Mountains, and entered the Holy Land. From there, he sent his report to Louis IX, who was then back in France. His Crusade in Egypt had ended with his capture by the Muslims in 1250. After being ransomed, he had spent four years in the Holy Land before returning to France.

William's descriptions of his travels to Karakorum and back are much more detailed than that of his predecessors. He wrote in great detail about the geography of the Mongol Empire as he traveled along the Silk Road. He also described the cultures and customs of the lands he passed through and characterized the conditions in Mongol military camps as appalling. "I can't find the words to tell you of the misery we suffered when we came to the encampments." The wretched conditions, wrote William, indicated that the Mongols would be no threat if the pope were to declare a Crusade against them.

Around the middle of the 13th century, information on the Mongol Empire was, despite the records of emissaries to the East, often incorrect or scant, and what little there was of it was not widely diffused. It is known that the fourth great khan, Möngke, renewed Mongol expansion. With his brother Kublai, he began to push into China. In the west, his younger brother Hülegü (ruler of the Ilkhanate from 1256 to 1265) invaded Iraq and took over the power of the Abbasid Caliphate. Hülegü moved into Syria and then conquered Aleppo and Damascus in 1260, receiving the vassalage of the Christian nobles in those cities. He was forced to retreat back to Azerbaijan upon hearing the news of the death of his brother, the great khan. The forces Hülegü left behind were defeated by the Mamluk sultan of Egypt, Saif ad-Din Qutuz, in the Battle of Ain Jalut near Galilee on September 3rd, 1260. It was this battle that ended the belief in the West that the Mongols were invincible.

While all of this was going on, the Silk Road had been traveled by a number of Europeans, almost exclusively emissaries of the Christian Church, who left records of their journeys. It is known that the journey to the East was accomplished by many others as well, primarily merchants, who did not leave records. The fact that European traders are mentioned in the accounts as being present in the East is not surprising, as for some time, under the auspices of the Mongol Empire, the Silk Road had evolved into something that resembles a modern highway—albeit with less traffic, of course.

It was in the last half of the 13th century that one of medieval Europe's most dazzling travelers left a record of his journey. Many readers will be familiar with the name of Marco Polo, who journeyed to the East along the Silk Road to visit the fabled court of the great khan. His host and employer in the East was none other than the warrior Kublai Khan, who expanded the Mongol Empire, lost the first major battles beyond the Mongol frontiers, and was the founder of a Chinese dynasty of emperors.

Chapter 8 – The Lord of Xanadu, Kublai Khan: The Emperor of China

The ascension to the throne of great khan by Genghis Khan's grandson, Kublai, who was in his forties, in 1260 marked the beginning of a new era in Mongol history. Not only did the Mongol Empire expand and become a highly organized imperial state, but it also reached a peak of sophistication before the empire began to crumble. It was the era when the land route from the West to the East along the Silk Road saw its highest level of activity before gradually being replaced by seaborne trade.

Kublai, who was born in 1215, was brought up under the tutelage of a Buddhist nursemaid. In his youth, he became enamored with Chinese culture. Because he was a minor princeling, just one among many in the extended family of descendants of Genghis Khan, he was not expected to have an important role. Kublai, in his youth, is mentioned here and there in the chronicles of his uncles and grandfather, *The Secret History of the Mongols*, which was written after the death of Genghis Khan. What little is recorded about

Kublai's youth is thanks to the widespread importance of his mother, Sorghaghtani Beki.

In order to pacify the rebellious Kerait steppe people, Genghis Khan arranged for his youngest son, Tolui, to marry Sorghaghtani, the daughter of the leader of the insurrectionist Kerait. This marriage alliance produced four sons, among whom was Kublai. Sorghaghtani, after the death of her husband, assumed power and promoted the religion of her family, Nestorian Christianity. Some in the West believed that it was her uncle who was the fabled Christian King Prester John. Whether Sorghaghtani's uncle was a Christian or not, it is unlikely that he would have traveled to the west with an army to assist the Crusaders.

Kublai Khan's ascent to the throne of the Mongol Empire was not simple. The matter of succession after Genghis Khan died was as one would expect in a newly formed empire—complicated. The great khan's Genghis's eldest son, Jochi, who seemed the most likely successor, predeceased his father, and his sons made no effort to assume power. Before dying, Genghis Khan had decreed that his third son, Ögedei, would succeed him if he was worthy. When Genghis died, his sons and grandsons fought to determine who was worthy of taking on the leadership of the Mongol Empire. Ögedei prevailed at a *kurultai*, or council meeting, and set about changing the administration in the Mongol Empire. In turning the more or less chaotic administration into something more civilized, Ögedei instituted a mounted postal system, built granaries, and instituted property taxes. The postal system, which worked through a kind of "pony express," required the construction of roads along which mounted couriers could cover as many as 250 miles a day. These roads also served to facilitate the transport of goods from one region to another.

Great Khan Ögedei, with the help of his family, including Kublai, attempted to stabilize territories outside Mongolia itself. By doing this, they ensured that the Mongols were sustained financially, thus alleviating the need for constant pillage of frontier lands in order to provide sufficient food for their people.

Ögedei further developed a spot marked out by his grandfather as a suitable Mongol capital, which Genghis Khan had named Karakorum or "Black Rock." It was there that Ögedei set up a town with four walls of rammed earth and an inner palace for the Mongol royals. Karakorum never did become a major city, but its adjacency to the Buddhist Erdene Zuu Monastery and its situation in the Orkhon Valley, which allowed them to be close to the Xiongnu and Uyghur peoples, permitted the establishment of a new centralized authority for the Mongol Empire. Mongol warlords set up encampments around the city, and Ögedei himself is said to have pulled up his portable palace there when he was not at war elsewhere. It was apparently a wagon ten meters (almost 33 feet) wide, drawn by 22 oxen.

From Karakorum, the Mongols controlled northern China through a kind of prime minister, a Chinese man named Yelü Chucai. The success of Yelü Chucai's management of China is indicated by the fact that he turned over around one thousand silver ingots of tax income in 1230. The importance of Karakorum in Mongol life, in spite of it being the capital, was minimal. According to Mongol custom, it was the duty of the youngest son of a warrior to remain at home and manage family affairs, primarily grazing the family livestock on what became overgrazed land. Elder sons were expected to go to war, pillage enemies, deal with revolts, and generally work to expand Mongol control everywhere. Ögedei, thus free from holding court in Karakorum, was at liberty to lead an army to attack northern Korea, which had stubbornly held off Mongol rule. Ögedei also dispatched an army to Iran to deal with the remaining Seljuk Turks there, and he led an army himself in regular incursions against China. A heavy drinker like most Mongols, Ögedei was stricken with a palsy, perhaps a stroke, that was brought on by intemperance. He was treated by shamans, who required the transference of the affliction to Tolui, Ögedei's younger brother. It is likely that the treatment involved the consumption of vast quantities of alcohol by Tolui, who died in the process in 1232. Ögedei, who was severely debilitated, continued to rule for another twenty years.

During those twenty years, Sorghaghtani, Tolui's wife, refused to remarry, which was the custom among the Mongols. She became the most powerful Mongol woman, having been bequeathed considerable land by her husband, which meant that she was both wealthy and powerful. Sorghaghtani's son, Kublai, was raised in a different environment than most Mongol warriors. Instead of following his father off to war, he led a sedentary life practicing hunting and the arts of war in the steppes around Karakorum. He was supplied with a Uyghur tutor from central Asia and learned how to read the Turkic script used by the Mongols.

Sorghaghtani, at some point, moved her family and court to the Hebei province in China. This was a territory that was rightfully hers since it had been conquered by her late husband. Hebei, however, was in ruins not only from the Mongol invasion but also because many of its residents had fled south into Song China to escape Mongol rule. More Chinese were forced to exit Hebei when the Mongols instituted punishing taxes on them. It is thought that the region, once home to forty million people, had been reduced to having around ten million inhabitants. Sorghaghtani's rule of Hebei was much more humane than the average Mongol control over other peoples. Sorghaghtani, as a Nestorian Christian, was tolerant and funded the establishments of other religions. Her administration also encouraged Chinese farmers to continue tilling the land. The conditions there were so amenable that some Chinese returned from the Song Empire in the south. By facilitating farming, Sorghaghtani was going against the Mongol custom of turning over captured farmland to nomadic herdsmen, who turned the once productive farms into pastures. In 1240, when her son Kublai was in his twenties, Sorghaghtani gave him the region of Jingzhou in southern Hubei on the banks of the Yangtze River. At first, Kublai neglected his estate, and it fell into ruin. Its tax income was stolen by agents of the Mongols and thus was not rendered to Kublai as it should have been. In an effort at reform, Kublai took a page from his mother's book of administration and regularized the management of his estate through Chinese agents, who were charged with reducing taxes and encouraging farming. The population of Jingzhou increased as the refugees returned to their lands.

When in 1241 Ögedei Khan finally drank himself to death, news of his demise eventually reached the West. Knowing that their leader would be summoned to a *kurultai* in Karakorum, the Mongol horde in Hungary retreated from the front, thus taking the pressure off Europe. Ögedei's wife, Töregene, began her unofficial reign while awaiting the convening of a *kurultai*; during her rule, there was religious friction among her advisors due to the overtaxation that was instituted by her Muslim tax collectors. None of this affected Kublai in his estates, which he ruled with some measure of magnanimity and unusual efficiency. Kublai's mother, the now very powerful Sorghaghtani, allied herself with the regent and Great Khatun Töregene, and it was believed that Sorghaghtani would be her ally in the deliberations of the *kurultai*. The meeting, which was held in 1246, settled the matter of succession to the throne by appointing Ögedei Khan's eldest son, Güyük, to the position.

A picture of the kind of housing that was common among the more elevated of the Mongols was reported on by Friar John of Plano Carpini, in which he described Töregene's tent at Karakorum at the time of the royal meeting. "After five or six days, he [Güyük] sent us to his mother [Empress Töregene], under whom there was maintained a very solemn and royal court. When we came there we saw a huge tent of fine white cloth, which was, in our judgement, so great that more than two thousand men might stand within it, and around about it there was set up a wall of planks, painted with diverse designs." Friar John described the conference of Mongols from as close as he could approach the tent housing the *kurultai*, observing the many dignitaries swarming around the entrance. "Without the door stood Duke Yaroslav of Susdal in Russia, and a great many dukes of the Cathayans, and of the Solands. The two sons also of the King of Georgia, an ambassador of the Caliph of Baghdad, who was a Sultan, and we think, more than ten other Sultans of the Saracens beside."

It is clear that by the time of this conference of royals and major and minor leaders of the Mongol Empire, travel along the Silk Road from had become if not commonplace, at least safe for parties who took the precaution of being accompanied by armed guards. Friar John claimed that some four thousand envoys, speaking many different languages from everywhere in the Mongol Empire, attended the coronation of the new Great Khan Güyük. It took place in a new camp set up some distance from Karakorum. In the center was, according to Friar John, an enormous tent called the Golden Orda. Unfortunately, on the date set for the momentous event, a destructive hailstorm hit, and the ceremonies were called off. A week later, within the confines of the Golden Orda, the princes of the royal family, among whom was Kublai, performed ritual submission before the new great khan. Immediately after the ceremony, Great Khan Güyük, possibly at the behest of his mother, held a show trial in which his aunts were accused of killing his father. They were summarily executed.

Friar John reported his own experience with the wrath of the new khan and his mother. He wrote that the Russian Duke Yaroslav was invited to a banquet with Töregene. "Immediately after the banquet, he fell sick, and within seven days he died. After his death, his body was of a strange blue color, and it was commonly reported that the duke had been poisoned." Accusations were leveled against the perceived enemies of the khan and his mother. It all came to an end when Güyük himself was assassinated or drank himself to death in 1248. It is possible that the great khan was poisoned by his brother Batu, who had been summoned to travel from the west to appear at the court in Karakorum. Any thought of reprisals against the khan's opposition ended with the death of Töregene, who died under suspicious circumstances in 1265, sometime after the enthronement of Kublai Khan.

Batu, who enjoyed his role in the west of the empire, called two *kurultais* of royals to elect a new khan. At the second one in 1251, Sorghaghtani's eldest son, Möngke (r. 1251-1259), was declared to be the great khan. A glimpse of the court of the Great Khan Möngke is given in William of Rubruck's account of his journey to the East. His audience with the great khan did not go well, as Möngke was distracted and drunk throughout their meeting. However, in his explorations of Karakorum, William met some interesting people. Among them was a woman named Paquette who came from Metz in France. She reported to him that she had been captured in Hungary and sent to Karakorum, where she became a slave of a Mongol warrior. She somehow escaped this horror and joined the entourage of a Mongol Christian princess. Paquette later married a Russian carpenter and had three children. William also reported on another Westerner who thrived in Karakorum, a Parisian goldsmith named William Bouchier, who had been captured in Europe and installed by Möngke as the head of a workshop with fifty artisans.

Great Khan Möngke's means of preventing domestic squabbles and revolts among the Mongol factions was to do what the Mongols had always done—conquer new lands. With his eyes on making further conquests in China, Möngke appointed one of his relatives who had shown great skill in pacifying the Chinese. He thus appointed Kublai viceregent over northern China, which Kublai ruled with great acumen, even managing to enlist Chinese warlords to assist him in wars. In 1253, Kublai was ordered to attack Yunnan in southwestern China. In this endeavor, he was remarkably successful. By 1256, he succeeded in pacifying Yunnan and placed it under Mongol control. In 1258, Kublai was put in charge of the eastern Mongol army and ordered to attack Sichuan. His method of approaching the province was unique. The Chinese had depopulated a vast swath of intervening territory so that any invading Mongol force would not be able to pillage enough food to take their army into China. Kublai countered this strategy by encouraging farmers to immigrate into the wasteland, providing them with seed and tools. He sent Chinese soldiers who had willingly joined his army into the fields to assist with the farming. He further instituted the use of paper currency, which facilitated trade along the frontiers and encouraged the migration of farmers into the region.

Kublai planned to defeat the Song Chinese, who were clinging to power in southern China, by outflanking them. In 1253, he moved into the Buddhist mountain kingdom of Dali, which straddled the upper reaches of the Yangtze, Mekong, and Salween Rivers. The Dali Kingdom lay on the major trading route from India to Annam (Vietnam). However, Kublai's envoys to the Dali court, who carried an offer of peace, were killed. According to Mongol custom, this was a capital offense that was deserving of the complete annihilation of the miscreant nation. Kublai was persuaded that this was not a useful approach to the people of Dali, though. Instead, he surrounded the Dali capital and demanded their capitulation. The king surrendered, and Kublai captured those responsible for the killing of his envoys, who were promptly put to death. The king of Dali, being innocent of the crime himself, was spared and left in charge of his city with a Mongol serving as his second-in-command. Kublai moved north from the defeated territory that the Mongols had named Yunnan, meaning south of the clouds. The slow conquest of the scattered hill tribes and the eventual incursion into Tibet was given to Kublai's general Uryangkhadai, who was also responsible for Mongol defeats in Annam (Vietnam). In 1257, Uryangkhadai proceeded as far as Hanoi, where he razed the city to the ground and forced the first emperor of the Trần dynasty, Trần Thái Tông to evacuate the capital. A counterattack led by Thái Tông was successful. The Mongol army, which was depleted by disease in a climate they were unused to, were forced to hurriedly leave Annam. Thái Tông then sent an embassy to the Great Khan Möngke, offering to deliver tribute on an annual basis, which more or less ceded Annam to the Mongols but only in a symbolic way.

Back in his lands in northern China, Kublai continued to follow a somewhat enlightened path, inspired by Chinese practices, in order to establish a stable state. He appointed Confucian scholars to his court and encouraged the hunting down of fortunetellers, who were a scourge according to Confucian orthodoxy. His ability to listen to the advice of his most prominent Confucian advisors and willingness to follow it became suspect in the Mongol capital of Karakorum, where Kublai was thought to be a traitorous Sinophile. He was, however, not entirely seduced by Chinese civilization, as he refused to institute the system of Chinese education and the Chinese system of examinations for positions in the public service. The reason for Kublai's refusal of the Chinese system was that he wanted to retain his Muslim tax collectors and use Nestorian Christian engineers. Further, Kublai would have been leery of heading a bureaucracy where Chinese, a language that he could only master in a rudimentary fashion, was the lingua franca.

When it came to subjugating the entirety of China, Kublai faced two opponents. In the north, the Jurchen people, who had originated in Manchuria and had founded the Jin dynasty. Despite their being conquered in 1234, they continued to present a danger in the form of a revolt. With the Jurchens pacified to a great extent, Kublai only faced the Southern Song in his ambitions to annex all of China into the Mongol Empire.

In order to cement his control over northern China, Kublai proposed building a palace there. A site some 170 miles north of modern Beijing was selected. The site was first named Kaiping, meaning open and flat, but was subsequently changed to Shangdu, or upper capital. The name would be mangled into several variants by Europeans, including Chandu and Xamdu. The latter name metamorphosed into what became the legendary Xanadu. Kublai's remarkable palace is best known to the modern world through the poem by Samuel Taylor Coleridge, written in 1797. It begins, "In Xanadu did Kubla Khan/A stately pleasure-dome decree." Kublai's palace was surrounded by an enormous park, where he exercised his passion for the hunt. In the park, Kublai was in the habit of staying in a yurt, the kind of tent in which his ancestors in Mongolia had lived.

Despite living a high life in his new palace, Kublai was still subservient to Great Khan Möngke. In fact, his accounts were audited by minions of the great khan. Finding irregularities in Kublai's books, several of his Chinese bureaucrats were executed.

Kublai went to his brother Möngke in Karakorum, and their differences were patched up in 1258. Möngke ordered Kublai to stay in his palace at Chandu while Möngke himself moved against the Southern Song at the head of a large army. The invasion did not go well, and Möngke was forced to call in his brother, who he acknowledged as a skilled commander.

At this time, the Mongol court almost collapsed due to infighting between the adherents of rival religions. Their numbers were constantly in flux with the arrivals and departures of religious people who moved along the Silk Road. With the fall of Tibet to Mongol control, Buddhists who were skilled in conjuring tricks seeped into Möngke's and Kublai's courts. They ran afoul of the Chan Buddhists (Zen Buddhists), who were already ensconced in the royal household, and were opposed by Taoists and Confucians, who adamantly opposed anything that smacked of sorcery. In the Mongol courts, on account of a policy of religious tolerance, religious debate was rife. In the 1250s, the Taoists claimed that Buddhism was no more than a sect of their own religion. They bolstered their case by citing the Taoist *Book of Barbarian Conversions*, or the *Huahujing*, which is said to have been written by Laozi, who lived sometime between the 6th to the 4th century BCE. It was said that Laozi traveled to India, where he regenerated into the Buddha. Buddhism was thus seen as merely a deluded form of Taoism. The Buddhist scholars at the great khan's court then backdated Buddha's life so that it predated any possible contact with Laozi, the founder of Taoism, and they declared Buddhism to be the only true religion. The religious dispute had real-world effects with differing religious communities despoiling their opponents' monasteries and temples. Möngke, recognizing Kublai's understanding of the Chinese way of doing things, appointed his brother to convene a debate between the Buddhists and Taoists. In 1258, the religious debate, with Kublai in the judge's chair, was held. Kublai, even though he seems to have adopted a Tibetan named Drogön Chögyal Phagpa as his personal guru, was in favor of the Buddhist argument. With the religious dispute in the Mongol courts settled, the Great Khan Möngke prepared to conquer the Southern Song once and for all. Möngke was to attack the Song from the west, and Kublai was to head south in the winter of 1258/1259 from Chandu with an army of 90,000 men.

In carrying out Genghis Khan's prophecy that the Mongols would rule the entire world, Möngke understood that his expedition would call for a non-Mongolian type of warfare. He enlisted Muslim engineers who had some familiarity with besieging cities in preparation for an attack on the largest urban cities in the world, such as Hangzhou, the temporary capital of the Southern Song, which had a population of around one and half million. While Kublai and his army swept south into Song territory, his brother Möngke got bogged down in fighting in the west. Möngke, although attempting to escape the disease-ridden west, fell victim to cholera and died in 1259 at the age of 51. Going against Mongol custom, which called for a retreat and a subsequent *kurultai* to appoint a new great khan, Kublai opted to continue his advance south across the Yangtze. An emissary from the Song offered to pay off the Mongols with an annual tribute of silver, carpets, fine silks, and brocades if they halted their advance.

At home in Karakorum, Kublai faced opposition. He was forced to retreat from his conquered Song lands and attend the Mongol *kurultai* to ensure that he ascended to the throne of great khan. Two conferences were held in 1260, and Kublai was declared as the next great khan at the first of these. The results were disputed, and a second *kurultai* was convened. The second elected Ariq Bök, Kublai's brother. Kublai's claim was bolstered by the arrival of emissaries from Korea, which was not yet completely subjugated. They swore fealty to Kublai and agreed to dismantle their defenses that had for so long held back Mongol invaders. Without even waging an all-out attack on Korea, Kublai had fortuitously added Korea to the Mongol Empire.

In the first stage of his civil war with his rival, Ariq Bök, for the title of great khan, Kublai cut off the trade routes that ran from Karakorum to the south, which supplied food to the Mongol capital. The dispute reached a climax in 1261 when, on a battlefield at the edge of the Gobi Desert, Ariq Bök's army was defeated by Kublai. The rebellious Bök continued to fight until it became clear to him that Kublai had the upper hand. The two reconciled in Chandu in 1264, but their amity was short-lived. Bök was placed on trial, but it was postponed soon after it started, as it required the attendance of the Mongol princes. Some of them were as far away as the Middle East, but their presence was necessary for a final *kurultai* that would definitively select the great khan. After two years in prison awaiting the convening of a full royal family conference, Bök died. Some suspected he was poisoned. Whatever actually happened, Kublai became the undisputed great khan.

Kublai's court, which had a majority of Chinese bureaucrats and advisors, took on the challenge of how Kublai Khan should rule the Mongol Empire. It may have been Kublai's preferred wife, Chabi, who encouraged him to emulate the administration of the ancient Chinese Tang Empire. Due to their infatuation with Tang China, Kublai and Chabi decided that the best way for the great khan to rule China was not as a Mongol conqueror. Rather, to ensure his hold on the Chinese part of his empire, Kublai would have to "go native" and adopt the Chinese way of government.

Among the allies of Kublai in the invasion of the Southern Song was Li Tan, an official in the Shandong province of Mongolia. He led an army south and was rewarded for his successes by being given the title of vice commander of an area of China the size of modern-day France. Although he was ordered not to move against the Southern Song, Li Tan proved to be victorious in several skirmishes with the Song. He turned against Kublai, who was then preoccupied with Ariq Bök. Li Tan turned his troops loose on the skeletal garrison of

Mongols in Shandong and ceded some fortified coastal cities to the Song. Kublai sent two generals to stamp out Li Tan's insurrection, and by the spring of 1262, Li Tan was arrested. It was reported that "When news came to the Great Khan, he was right well pleased, and ordered that all the chiefs who had rebelled, or excited others to rebel, should be put to a cruel death." Li Tan was put in a sack and trampled to death by Mongol horsemen. A confederate of Li Tan and the Song was discovered in Kublai's court, and he, too, was executed. The effect of this rebellion in Shandong was a lessening of the great khan's enthusiasm for the Chinese way of administration. He turned to using officials from non-Chinese cultures, such as the Italian Marco Polo, who took a civil service job in a Chinese city.

Although he may have soured on the Chinese style of government, Kublai understood the importance of the way he managed his Chinese territories. In the north, he wanted to appear sympathetic to Chinese interests so as not to alarm the Song Chinese, who were on the verge of being forced into the Mongol Empire. The management of the Chinese needed to be handled delicately because, in the north, the Mongols were outnumbered, perhaps by a margin of five to one. If Kublai assumed control of southern China, with a population in the range of forty million, the scarcity of Mongols to keep order would become critical. So, he set about putting advice from his Confucian advisors into practice. They proposed that Kublai always present a magnanimous face. If he was effective in winning the hearts and minds of the Song, they would, without warfare, beg to be permitted to enter the Mongol Empire.

An emissary was sent by Kublai to the Song, who pleaded for their complete submission to Mongol authority. The ambassador painted Kublai as a virtual Chinese man who would make few changes to the organization of the Song bureaucracy. The most important difference would be that taxes would flow to the great khan and not the leader of the Song Empire. Kublai promised to ensure that Song merchants would not be harassed in the north, insisting that their trade route would continue as it had in the past when the north was under

Chinese domination. In spite of this, there were continual tensions on the Yangtze River, the border between the Mongols and the Song. It was actually Kublai's Mongol heart, full as it was with traditional Mongol expansionist notions, that won him over. Kublai prepared for a major invasion of the south, following the Mongol tradition of expansionism to generate wealth, to gather new slaves to put to work, and to focus the attention of subjects on outward goals. It was his intention to settle dealings with the Song by taking over their territory.

The invasion of the south involved a difficult transition in the Mongol means of warfare. While Kublai's army was adept on the flatlands of the steppes, they were untrained in slogging through the wet rice fields of the south, surviving intense heat, and fending off tropical diseases. The challenge of finding enough grazing land for the Mongol horses and the unprecedented need to deal with shipborne fighters that were fielded by the Song weighed heavily on Kublai Khan. In order to cross the Yangtze effectively and to patrol the coastline of Song China, Kublai needed a navy. The beginning of this enterprise was the capture of 146 Song ships that had sailed up the Yangtze almost as far as Sichuan. These ships were put to use by Kublai in his attack in 1268 on Xiangyang (in the modern-day Hubei province) on the Han River. Even though it was surrounded by Mongol forts, food and soldiers made it into the city, providing relief for the inhabitants inside. The siege went on and on. A major delivery of supplies to the besieged city came when two thousand Song soldiers smashed the Mongol blockade on the Han River. The Mongol siege was, in a sense, professionalized when experts in siege warfare arrived from Persia. These engineers built huge trebuchets, or mangonels, that were capable of throwing a 300-pound rock over the walls of the city. Using these devices, the Mongols pounded the walls of Xiangyang into rubble. The historical sources are unclear as to whether the builders of the mangonels were, in fact, Persians. One source claims the engineers were from Damascus, where familiarity with the effectiveness of mangonels was obtained from the sieges of Crusader castles. In his book about his visit to Kublai Khan, the

Italian merchant Marco Polo went so far as to claim that the mangonel builders were himself, his father, his uncle, and some unnamed assistants. "Then spoke up the two brothers and Messer Marco the son, and said: 'Great Prince, we have with us among our followers men who are able to construct mangonels which shall cast such great stones that the garrison will never be able to stand them, but surrender." The boasting of this deed has much to do with Polo's entire account of his stay in China being seen as a false narrative. When the siege of Xiangyang occurred, the Polos were not even in China.

Xiangyang finally fell to the Mongols in 1272 after a five-year siege. In order to consolidate the command of his expeditionary force, Kublai appointed General Bayan to be the supreme commander. He marched his troops down the Yangtze and laid siege to Hangzhou. His army was bolstered with the addition of many Song Chinese turncoats who understood that trade with the Mongols would eventually be conducted with respect.

The Song Chinese, at the time of the siege, were led by Empress Dowager Quan and Grand Empress Dowager Xie. The latter was a very strong advocate for the Song cause; at one point, she egged on her supporters, proclaiming, "Since ancient times there has not yet been an age of total barbarian conquest. How has it come to this present state that deviates from the constants of Heaven and Earth." In spite of her bluster, at the end of 1275, Xie was forced to turn over the imperial seal to Bayan, ceding the Song capital to him. The four-year-old heir to the Song dynasty was packed off to the south. He was eventually apprehended by the Mongols and sent to a monastery in Tibet.

Even before the fall of Hangzhou, Kublai declared himself to be the emperor of China. He chose the name for his dynasty carefully so as not to emphasize its "barbarian" origin and antagonize the population. So, in a brilliant move, he established the Yuan dynasty. Kublai sent letters to the peoples on the periphery of his new Chinese empire. From the king of Korea, he received strong support since the

Mongol troops had been instrumental in putting down an insurrection against the king. He wrote to the Japanese and the king of Annam, expecting them to swiftly acknowledge his role as Ruler of All Under Heaven. In both cases, the authorities dragged their feet.

Meanwhile, the great khan busied himself in creating a capital fit for the new emperor of China.

Chapter 9 – Marco Polo Visits Kublai Khan's China

While conquering the southern Chinese and subsequently founding the Yuan Dynasty in 1279, Kublai Khan had to deal with unrest in the far reaches of his empire. In Mongolia, he was constantly threatened by internal warfare. In the west of the Mongol Empire, unrest swept the rulership of the Golden Horde. Kublai's administrators were pushed aside in a civil war, and the armies of the Golden Horde and those of the Mongol khanate in Persia, known as the Ilkhanate, clashed. In this period of internal strife, traders from the Latin West made inroads in commerce with nearby parts of the Mongol Empire. By 1263, western merchants were established in Tabriz, the leading commercial center of Persia. Under Hulagu Khan, the ruler of the Ilkhanate from 1256 to 1265, and his successor Abaqa Khan, who reigned from 1265 to 1282, the relations between the Christian West and Persia improved. Abaqa had a Christian mother, and among his wives was the daughter of Byzantine Emperor Michael VIII Palaeologus. This meant that Christian missionaries, diplomats, and merchants became prominent in the city of Tabriz. Attempts were made to improve diplomacy between the court of Abaqa and the West, among which was the failed coordination of Persian military action and the Crusade of Prince Edward of England between 1270 and 1272.

The primary source of information on what lay to the east of Europe during the first half of the 14th century was a book entitled *The Travels of Marco Polo* or the *Book of the Marvels of the World*, dating from around 1300. Most of what surrounds this account of Polo's journey to the East is shrouded in mystery, and the truth of its contents has been subject to debate.

In the 1250s, Venetian merchants Niccolò and Maffeo Polo ran a trading business shipping goods from the East to Venice, where they were then transported to European markets. The Polos operated out of the Crimean port of Soldaia (modern-day Sudak). Their major competition came from Venetian trading enterprises operating from Constantinople, which was the center of the Latin Empire, which stretched from the Balkans to the Levant. Among the exotic trade goods that flowed from the East into Constantinople and dependent ports were silk, dyes, furs, pepper, cotton, and slaves. It was to Crimea that Russians delivered amber, honey, wax, and furs. The most important of the Polos trade was in foodstuffs originating in the European steppes.

According to the book that became known as *The Travels of Marco Polo*, Niccolò and Maffeo Polo set out in 1260 to trade jewels with the merchants of the Golden Horde in Russia. They traveled to Sarai (near present-day Volgograd), where they met and exchanged goods with the grandson of Genghis Khan, Berke Khan, who reigned over the Golden Horde from 1257 to 1266. Because the archenemy of Venice, Genoa, in league with the Byzantines, reconquered Constantinople in 1261, the Polos avoided returning to Venice through Byzantine territory. They might have wished to travel south from Russia through Georgia and Armenia to Tabriz, the capital of the Ilkhanate, but this route home became impossible because a war had broken out between Berke Khan of the Golden Horde and Hulagu, the Mongol khan of Persia. Apparently, the Polos left Sarai and headed directly east, crossing a desert in central Asia to arrive at

Bukhara, located in present-day Uzbekistan. There, they were convinced by an emissary from the Persian Ilkhan Hulagu, who was on his way to see the great khan, that they should join him. According to the book, the Polo brothers traveled a year north and northeast until they arrived at the court of Kublai Khan.

The great khan gave them letters in Mongolian to deliver to the pope. He asked the pope to send him one hundred teachers of the liberal arts who could convert the Mongols to Catholicism. The actual nature of this request seems to have been more along the lines of the great khan needing the assistance of European administrators to deal with the Chinese in the north, who Kublai was on the verge of conquering. Kublai Khan also asked that the Polos secure for him some oil from the lamp of the Holy Sepulcher in Jerusalem and have it sent to him. To facilitate their journey west to their home in Venice, the Polo brothers were given a pass that entitled them to pass through all of the Mongol lands without hindrance. After a journey that was said, although most likely in exaggeration, to have lasted three years, they reached the port of Layas or Aegeae (now the Turkish holiday town of Yumurtalik) and sailed off to Acre and from there sailed home to Venice. In Venice, Niccolò was reunited with his son Marco, who the book says was fifteen years old at the time.

Three years later, the Polo brothers decided to visit the great khan, and they took Niccolò's young son Marco with them. They sailed to Acre and then visited Jerusalem to secure the sacred oil as requested by the great khan. Returning to Acre, they learned that Archdeacon Tedaldo Visconti, then in residence there, had just been elected as Pope Gregory X (pontiff from 1271 to 1276).

The new pope, instead of sending a group of educators or administrators to Kublai Khan as requested, provided the Polo merchant expedition with two Dominican friars, Brother Niccolò of Vicenza and Brother William of Tripoli. They were, according to *The Travels of Marco Polo*, endowed by the pope with "the necessary authority, that they might do everything in those countries with full powers, ordain priests and consecrate bishops...He [the pope] gave them written credentials and letters, and entrusted them with the message he wished to send to the Great Khan." The journey to the court of the great khan took three and a half years, which Marco Polo said was "owing to the bad weather and severe cold they encountered." They arrived in Karakorum in 1275. There, they "went to the Royal Palace, where they found the Great Khan surrounded by a large company of barons. So, they kneeled before him and paid him their respects in the humblest possible manner...They presented the credentials and letters the Pope sent him, which pleased him exceedingly. They then consigned the holy oil, over which he rejoiced very much."

Marco described Kublai Khan in the book, saying, "He is of good stature, neither tall nor short, but of a middle height. He has a becoming amount of flesh, and is very shapely in all his limbs. His complexion is white and red, the eyes black and fine, the nose well formed and well set on."

The Polos were to spend the next seventeen years in the East. Although there are no Chinese records to confirm this, according to the record of the Polos' travels, Kublai Khan used young Marco as an administrator.

> Now it happened that Marco, the son of Messer Niccolò, learnt so well the customs, languages and manners of writing of the Tartars, that it was truly a wonder, for I tell you in sooth that, not long after he had reached the Court of the Great Lord, he knew four languages, and their alphabets, and manner of writing. He was exceedingly wise and prudent, and the Great Khan loved him very much.

In 1273, Kublai completed his conquest of China, thus reuniting both northern and southern China. Marco Polo seems to have served the great khan as an ambassador to far-off regions of the Mongol Empire, reporting back with descriptions of the peoples and what he saw. The Polos, who had asked permission to return to Europe on several occasions but were rebuffed by the great khan, were at last chosen to accompany an imperial princess on her journey to marry

Arghun Khan. After an arduous voyage, the princess was delivered to the khan's court in Persia. The three Polos traveled west through Trebizond on the Black Sea to Constantinople and arrived home in Venice in 1295. Marco was, at the time, 41 or 42 years of age.

At some point, under circumstances that are unknown, Marco was captured at sea by the Genoese. He was thrown into prison where, apparently, he wrote the account of his travels to the East. Marco was released and, in 1299, returned home to Venice. Marco's manuscript for his book on his travels was copied by scribes and translated into several European languages, and Marco was consulted by scholars on the subjects of geography and the peoples of the East.

The co-author of *The Travels of Marco Polo*, Rustichello da Pisa, was with Marco in prison in Genoa. The flourishes of romance included in the travel book and the way the story is framed have been attributed to Rustichello. It is for this reason that one should doubt every statement in the book as being entirely factual. Scholars have debated whether indeed the book was dictated by Marco Polo himself, and they have also disputed over the input of copyists of the text, as the original has disappeared. Furthermore, scholars have found it difficult to determine the locations of many of the places mentioned in the text. It is believed that Marco Polo and Rustichello da Pisa often used place names that were poorly translated from local languages. Considering some of Polo's observations, whether accurate or not, is valuable in understanding what kind of information was spread in Europe regarding the previously unrecorded path to the East and the wonders of China.

Marco Polo described the city of Mosul as he observed it in the late 13th century. He reported that in Mongol-controlled Mosul, Christians of various sects and Muslims intermingled freely. He noted that the Muslims manufactured silk cloths and that they "convey spices and drugs, in large quantities, from one country to another." In the mountains north of Mosul, said Polo, "there is a race of people named Kurds...They are an unprincipled people, whose occupation is to rob merchants."

In Baghdad, the Venetian merchant wrote, that "there is a manufacture of silks wrought with gold, and also of damasks, as well as of velvets ornamented with figures of birds and beasts." In Taurus in Iraq, "the inhabitants support themselves principally by commerce and manufactures, which latter consist of various kinds of silk, some of them interwoven with gold, and of high price." From this, we can learn that silk, perhaps even the bulk of it, moving along the Silk Road to the West was not manufactured by the Chinese. Taurus was an important trading center, where, "The merchants from India...as well as from different parts of Europe, resort thither to purchase and sell a number of articles." As a good Christian, Marco Polo could not resist opining on the Muslims, the dominant group of Taurus. He said that according to their doctrine, whatever was stolen or plundered from others of a different faith was now theirs, and the theft would be not be seen as a crime.

While in Persia, Marco Polo inquired the locals about the origin of the three Magi, who brought exotic gifts to the infant Jesus. He recorded the story in his book, along with other regional legends. He encountered Yazidis in Persia and noted that they made "a species of cloth of silk and gold...known by the appellation of Yasti." This cloth was "carried from thence by the merchants to all parts of the world." Marco Polo tells of the city-state of Ormus (Hormuz), where the temperatures forced the inhabitants to retreat in the summer to houses that had been constructed over a river. This was probably hearsay that Marco Polo had obtained through imperfect translation. It is likely that this reference to houses on a river, in fact, concerned the forced evacuation of the people of Ormuz to the island of Hormuz, who were pushed out by the Muslim Kerman Seljuk Sultanate or by the Mongol invaders.

In Timochain, located in the Fars Province of northern Persia, Marco Polo records that he learned of the legend of the Old Man of the Mountain, including his band of assassins and his base in the city of Balach that was destroyed by the Mongols. Balach, says Marco Polo, "contained many palaces constructed of marble, and spacious squares, still visible, although in a ruinous state." In this part of the story of his travels, Marco Polo describes Kashmir, although it is unlikely that he went there.

Reaching Kotan on the southern route of the Silk Road around the Taklamakan Desert, Marco Polo says that the people there were mostly Muslims. We know today that Polo's observation was incorrect because Khotan was, at the time, a Buddhist state within the Mongol Empire. Khotan, said Polo, "yields cotton, flax, hemp, grain, wine and other articles. The inhabitants cultivate farms and vineyards and have numerous gardens. They support themselves also by trade and manufactures, but they are not good soldiers."

When he came to the Lop Desert, in what is today the home of the Muslim Uyghurs in Xinjiang in the far northwest of China, Polo records that the region, which was under the dominion of the great khan, was populated with Muslims. Travelers who intended to cross the desert, said Polo, "usually halt for a considerable time at this place [the town of Lop], as well to repose from their fatigues as to make the necessary preparations for their further journey. For this purpose, they load a number of stout asses and camels with provisions and with their merchandise...Camels are commonly here employed in preference to asses, because they carry heavy burdens and are fed with a small quantity of provisions. The stock of provisions should be laid in for a month, that time being required for crossing the desert in the narrowest part."

In the part of his tale when Polo gets to Karakorum, the former capital of the Mongol Empire, he relates the story of how Genghis Khan marched against Prester John, who was encamped on the great plain of Tenduk. After receiving good omens for the outcome of the battle, the Mongols launched an attack. The Mongol army broke through Prester John's ranks and entirely routed the enemy. "Prester John himself was killed, his kingdom fell to the conqueror, and Genghis Khan espoused his daughter."

The Great Khan's palace in Shandu (Chandu or Xanadu), says Polo, had halls and chambers all in gilt. The palace was "contained within a wall to enclose sixteen miles in circuit of the adjoining plain. It contains the Royal Park with trees and birds. The number of these birds is upwards of two hundred, without counting the hawks." In the midst of the park, there was a royal pavilion in the form of a yurt.

> It is gilt all over, most elaborately finished inside and decorated with beasts and birds of very skillful workmanship. It is supported upon a colonnade of handsome pillars, gilt and varnished. Round each pillar a dragon, likewise gilt, entwines its tail, whilst its head sustains the projection of the roof, and its talons or claws are extended to the left and right...The construction of the pavilion is so devised that it can be taken down and put up again quickly; and it can be taken to pieces and removed wherever the Emperor may command. When erected, it is braced by more than 200 chords of silk.

Polo then gives a description of Kublai's successful battle against the rebellious Mongol Prince Nayan. This may be a firsthand report of the event that took place in July of 1287. "Kublai took his station in a large wooden castle, borne on the backs of four elephants, whose bodies were protected with coverings of thick leather hardened by fire, over which were housings of cloth of gold. The castle contained many crossbow-men and archers." In *The Travels of Marco Polo*, Kublai Khan's army is said to have "consisted of thirty battalions of horse, each battalion containing ten thousand men." After his victory, Kublai Khan returned to Khanbalu (Beijing) in November.

At Easter the following year, Kublai Khan told the Christians to "attend to him" and to bring their Bible. Marco Polo recorded the following about it in his book.

> After causing it [the Bible] to be repeatedly perfumed with incense, in a ceremonious manner, he devoutly kissed it, and directed that the same should be done by all his nobles who were present. This was his usual practice upon each of the principal Christian festivals...He observed the same at the festivals of the Saracens [Muslims], Jews and idolaters. Upon being asked his motive for this conduct, he said: "There are

four great Prophets who are reverenced and worshipped by the different classes of mankind...I do honor and show respect to all four"...But from the manner in which his majesty acted toward them, it is evident that he regarded the faith of the Christians as the right one and the best; nothing, as he observed, being enjoined to its professors that was not filled with virtue and holiness.

Whether this was true or not, it should be understood that Polo was writing for a Christian audience.

One of the customs of the great khan that clearly astonished Marco Polo involved his choice of marital partners.

> When his majesty is desirous of the company of one of his empresses, he either sends for her, or goes himself to her palace. Besides these, he has many concubines provided for his use from a province of Tartary named Ungut [possibly in modern-day Iran], the inhabitants of which are distinguished for beauty of features and fairness of complexion. Every second year, or oftener, as it may happen to be his pleasure, the Great Khan sends thither his officers, who collect for him, one hundred or more, of the handsomest of the young women, according to the estimation of beauty communicated to them in their instructions.

Marco Polo was present during the construction of Kublai Khan's royal palace and Chinese capital in Beijing. One of the buildings that impressed him was an observatory constructed in the 1270s.

> They have a kind of astrolabe on which are inscribed the planetary signs, the hours and critical points of the whole year. Every year the Christian, Saracen and Chinese astrologers, each sect apart, investigate by means of this astrolabe the course and character of the whole year...in order to discover by the natural course and disposition of the planets, and the other circumstances of the heavens...what shall be the nature of the weather, and what peculiarities shall be produced by each Moon of the year.

This astonishing scientific procedure was something quite foreign in Europe, and thus it fascinated the visiting Marco Polo. He was likewise in awe over the great khan's project for his new capital, saying that "All the plots of ground on which the houses of the city are built are four-square and laid out with straight lines...Each square plot [in Beijing] is encompassed by handsome streets for traffic, and thus the whole city is arranged in squares just like a chess-board." This was, of course, nothing like the medieval cities of Europe, where topography and traditional paths determined the siting of housing plots. Marco Polo left Beijing before the renovation and extension of the Grand Canal, linking Beijing and Hangzhou, was completed. This engineering feat would certainly have impressed him. Marco Polo also missed the completion of the elaborate system of water supply and lake extension in the north of the city. Because no Westerner would have been allowed within a stone's throw of Kublai's palace itself, it was only described by those who climbed a hill overlooking the structure. Friar Odoric of Pordenone, who visited Beijing after Marco Polo, wrote of the palace in rather vague terms. "In the city, the great emperor Khan has his principal seat, and his imperial palace, the walls of which palace are four miles in circuit." One of Kublai's major contributions to the cityscape of Beijing was the restoration of the 11th-century Great White Pagoda. This Buddhist structure was the tallest building in Beijing.

The objects of trade that reached Beijing were all subject to the monopoly of the great khan. Marco Polo noted the following:

> Furthermore, all merchants arriving from India or other countries, and bringing with them gold or silver or gems and pearls, are prohibited from selling to any one but the Emperor. He has twelve experts chosen for this business, men of shrewdness and experience in such affairs; these appraise the articles, and the Emperor then pay a liberal price for them in those pieces of paper [paper currency].

While Kublai was not the first to use paper currency, his use of this kind of commerce was widespread enough to intrigue Marco Polo.

He reported that the money was made from the tough bark of the mulberry tree and was treated with great respect. It was a legal tender whose use was enforced by the law. If a merchant refused to accept it as payment, he was subject to execution. When notes became too damaged to be used, merchants could swap them at the imperial treasury on payment of a 3 percent fee.

Marco Polo said of the khan's finances, "Now you have heard the ways and means whereby the Great Khan may have, and in fact has, more treasure than all the Kings in the World; and you know all about it and the reason why." Of course, the use of paper money inevitably resulted in inflation.

There was, at this time, other contacts established between the East and the West. Under the patronage of Kublai Khan, two Nestorian monks, Rabban Sauma and Rabban Mark, undertook a pilgrimage west to Jerusalem. Both of these monks were of Turkish or Uyghur origin. Their route took them along the Silk Road, passing Khotan, Kashgar, and Azerbaijan, and arriving in Baghdad in 1280. Here, the patriarch of the Nestorian Church appointed Rabban Mark as the Nestorian Metropolitan of Cathay and Ong (Shanxi). When the patriarch died, Rabban Mark was appointed, probably at the command of Kublai Khan, to be the new patriarch of the Nestorian Church. Rabban Sauma, in 1287, was sent on by Arghun Khan to head an embassy to Europe. He was accompanied by two Italians, Tommaso, a member of a Genoese banking family, and Ughetto, who was to act as an interpreter. They went to Rome and Genoa, met with King Philip IV in Paris, and celebrated Christian communion with Edward I of England in Bordeaux. Rabban Sauma went back to Rome, where he met with Pope Nicholas IV and delivered an invitation from Arghun Khan to send Catholic missionaries to the court of the Great Khan Kublai.

The pope commissioned the Franciscan friar John of Montecorvino to travel to China in response to Kublai Khan's request. John set out in 1289 in the company of Dominican Friar Nicholas of Pistoia and a merchant, Peter of Lucalongo. It was clearly the intention that land-based commerce along the Silk Road would be an important byproduct of converting the Chinese. The mission followed a circuitous route to the court of the great khan. After stopping in Tabriz, the capital of the Ilkhanate in Persia, Montecorvino and his companions sailed to Madras in India in 1291. He then went by sea from Bengal to China, where he appeared in Khanbaliq (modern-day Beijing) in 1294. Although Kublai Khan had died and the Mongol Empire was ruled by his successor, Temür Khan (r. 1294–1307), John was welcomed by the new great khan and the rulers of the Chinese puppet state of the Mongols known as the Yuan dynasty.

John built two churches in Khanbaliq and set up Christian workshops, which he populated with young boys he had bought from their heathen parents. He had the boys instructed in Latin and Greek and trained them in the rites and traditions of the Catholic Church. He taught himself the Uyghur language, which was the common tongue of the Mongol rulers in China, and translated the New Testament and Psalms into Uyghur. John's success involved the conversion of hundreds of Chinese-Mongols and earned him the wrath of Nestorian Christians, who were quite numerous in the territories controlled by the Mongols in Yuan China. Christian reinforcements were sent to John in 1307, but of the seven Franciscans who set out from Europe, only three arrived in China. As instructed by the pope, they consecrated John as the archbishop of Beijing. Among the high points reported in John's mission was the conversion of the great khan to Catholicism, who, at the time, was Külüg (r. 1307–1311) and known as Emperor Wuzong of the Yuan dynasty. However, there is some doubt as to the truth of this claim. It is thought that John of Montecorvino died in Beijing around 1328 because, in a letter from 1336 from Toghon Temür, who became the emperor of the Yuan dynasty in 1333, it was reported that the Chinese Mongol khanate had lacked a spiritual leader for the eight years since John's death. The letter was delivered by an embassy sent from Mongol China headed by Andrea di Nascio, a Genoese in the court of Toghon Temür. Di Nascio was accompanied by another Genoese merchant, Andalò di Savignone. The presence of trusted Genoese in the court in China indicates that by this time, there was significant commerce between the East and the West.

The pope maintained an interest in the affairs of the Christian Church in China. In 1338, he sent fifty ecclesiastics to the Mongol khanate in China. The absence of religious prejudice among the Mongols allowed for the prosperity of the Christian Church in Yuan China. This all came to an end, though, in 1368, when the Chinese rose up and overthrew their Mongol overlords. In the early years of the Ming dynasty, which lasted from 1368 to 1644, all of the Christians were expelled from China.

Marco Polo, throughout his many travels, visited many large and small cities in Yuan China. Most of those named in his book cannot be connected with any degree of certainty to specific Chinese cities. One that can, however, is Kin Sai, which has been identified as Hangzhou, which, it is said, that Marco Polo visited frequently. Hangzhou, it is stated, is a hundred miles in circumference, "its streets and canals are extensive, and there are squares and market-places...[where] officers appointed by the Great Khan are stationed, to take immediate notice of any differences that may happen to arise between the foreign merchants..." Canals "run through every quarter of the city" and are crossed by twelve thousand bridges. Around part of the city was a ditch that served to divert flooding rivers and functioned as a defensive moat when necessary. Marco Polo was impressed by the markets of Hangzhou, which he described in detail, noting, in particular, the delicious peaches and pears. He also seems to have been attracted by the courtesans who lived in a special quarter of Hangzhou. "These women," he said, "are accomplished, and are perfect in the arts of caressing and fondling which they accompany with expressions adapted to every description of person."

The extensive description of Hangzhou and its inhabitants by Marco Polo suggests that it was his favorite of all the cities he visited in China. He took great interest in the recreation afforded by the lake in

Hangzhou, describing in detail the vessels in which the locals amused themselves "either in the company of their women or that of their male companions." The people of Hangzhou, said Marco Polo, "think of nothing else" after their days of labor than "passing the remaining hours in parties of pleasure, with their wives or their mistresses."

Chapter 10 – The Final Years of Kublai Khan

The defeat of the remaining Song came about in a naval battle near Xinhui (in modern-day Guangdong) in the Battle of Yamen, which was fought on March 19th, 1279. With the demise of the remnants of the Song administration, Kublai Khan could, in truth, claim to be the emperor of a China that was unified for the first time in centuries. Rather than attempt to expand Mongol rule in the south into Vietnam, Kublai Khan turned his attention to Japan, the most important kingdom in the Far East that had yet to fall under Mongol control.

In his plan to subjugate Japan, the kingdom of Korea had to be called upon to provide military resources. This was the price that King Wonjong (ruled off and on between 1260 and 1274) had to pay for agreeing to subject his country to Mongol authority. Thus, he and his successors served as the great khan's agents in fighting with Japan. After a series of raids on Japan and preemptive attacks by Japan on the coast of Korea, Kublai sent an embassy to Japan in 1266, demanding that the nation submit to the Ruler of the World. He also sent a letter to King Wonjong of Korea, demanding that Korean warriors act as his proxies in an invasion of Japan. The Koreans obfuscated, though, and Kublai responded with a demand that they cooperate with his expansionist plan. He wrote to the king of Korea, "As to the Japanese matter, we shall leave it entirely in your hands, and we desire your Highness to bide by our wishes and convey our message to Japan, resting only when the end is attained without mishap." He also wrote to the emperor of Japan, who he addressed as "the king of a little country," saying, "We desire to remind you that Korea is now one of our eastern provinces, and that Japan is a mere appendage of Korea." This letter was ignored, as were representatives from Korea. A Korean ambassador to Kublai's court attempted to dissuade the great khan from his designs on Japan. Kublai said that the Japanese were presumptuous, even to the level of calling their leader emperor of the Land of the Rising Sun. Further, said the ambassador, the rumor that Japan was extraordinarily wealthy was, in fact, overblown. His last piece of advice to the great khan outlined the difficulties and dangers of a seaborne assault on Japan. The ambassador was doing his best to protect the interests of Korea, as it was expected that any Mongol invasion of Japan would be carried out, for the most part, by Korean mariners and soldiers. He failed to convince Kublai, though, who ordered that Korea construct one thousand ships and fill them with four thousand bags of rice and man them with forty thousand troops.

After sending three missions to Japan, none of which got farther than the island of Tsushima in the Korean Strait, Kublai sent a trusted advisor to Japan. Upon reading the great khan's demand that Japan subject itself to his authority, the ambassador was ejected from Japan. Kublai might well have abandoned his designs on Japan, but the arrogance of the Japanese in rejecting any notion of friendship with the Yuan emperor of China, coupled with the need in the Mongol Empire to project absolute strength, forced Kublai to invade Japan.

In 1274, a fleet of Korean ships carrying fifteen thousand Korean, Mongol, and Jurchen soldiers set out from the port of Pusan. The armada stopped at the island of Tsushima and launched an assault on the local samurai. The samurai, who were trained to conduct war in a ritual fashion, soon fell to the Mongol assault of poisoned arrows and ungentlemanly mass violence. The samurai, overwhelmed by the superior numbers, retreated, and they, along with the civilian inhabitants of Tsushima, were massacred. The same thing happened when the massive fleet landed on the island of Iki. To throw terror into the hearts of those on the sparsely defended island, the ships had their prows decorated with the captured dead or dying naked women, whose bodies, according to the annals of the Yuan dynasty, were affixed with nails through their palms. Pushing their lines forward behind a mass of captured Japanese women, the Mongols succeeded in overtaking the entire island.

The Mongol fleet soon moved on to Hakata Bay on the island of Kyūshū, a natural place for an amphibious assault. The samurai on this island were better prepared than those of the other Japanese islands. The Japanese knights held back the Mongol onslaught, and the Mongol forces retreated to their ships at the end of the day's fighting. A conference aboard the Mongol flagship was indecisive of whether the Japanese would attack before moonrise and whether the Mongols should mount a counterattack on land immediately. The samurai struck first. In more than three hundred tiny boats, they surrounded the Mongol fleet and pushed fireboats against the enemy ships. Fire on the vessels, whose holds had been kept dry to preserve gunpowder, spread quickly, and some vessels exploded. The Mongol ship captains attempted to move their vessels out to the open sea, where they expected to be able to ride out the destructive storm that had suddenly moved into Hakata Bay. However, the Mongol fleet was destroyed in the violent storm, with only a few ships surviving to retreat to Korea. What became known as the Battle of Bun'ei or the First Battle of Hakata Bay on November 19th, 1274, became the stuff of legend in Japan, as the victory over the Mongols was attributed not only to the superiority of the samurai warriors but also to divine intervention with the arrival of a storm at a critical moment in the conflict.

Following the Mongol defeat, Kublai Khan sent an emissary to Japan. The ambassador made the mistake of calling the Japanese emperor a king and said that the leader of the Mongols was a great emperor. Emperor Hōjō Tokimune (r. 1268-1284) dismissed the Mongol offer of peace. He said in no uncertain terms to Kublai's ambassador, "Listen, Mongol. Whosoever threatens a peaceful nation or tribe with the object of confiscating its resources...is without doubt a robber." And he added that since the time of Genghis Khan, "not a single day has been spent in peaceful rule, but the east and west have been terrorized by the Khan's brutal acts." The audience went from bad to worse, and the envoys of Kublai were executed. It is likely that Emperor Tokimune's fierce resistance to the Mongols was a result of the unrest in Japan caused by a popular Buddhist sect foretelling the end of the world. This doomsday prognostication was something that the bravest of samurai would have thought to be unthinkable.

Because the murder of ambassadors was anathema to the Mongol code of ethics, Kublai sent out orders to Korea that a second armada must be prepared. A further directive was delivered to Kublai's administrators in Yangzhou on the Grand Canal. One of the public servants in Yangzhou was Marco Polo, and he recorded the massive undertaking there to construct fifteen thousand ships "to carry his [the great khan's] armies to the isles of the sea." He said that each of the transport ships would have a crew of twenty and carry fifteen horses with their riders and provisions. It was through the writings of Marco Polo that the West first learned of Japan, although he called the country "Cipangu" and what he said of it was entirely based on Kublai's invasion. Working from imperial Mongol propaganda, Polo stated that Japan was a country of immense wealth, having much gold and pearls in abundance. The Japanese emperor's palace was, said Polo, "entirely roofed with fine gold," and the floors throughout the palace were paved in gold "in plates like slabs of stone, a good two fingers thick."

The Yangzhou fleet under the command of the Mongol general Arkham and the Korean fleet left their home ports in June 1281.

When they finally met up in Hakata Bay in August, the fighters, which included Koreans, Mongols, and Chinese, were in poor condition on account of disease and exhaustion. Their supplies were dwindling, and their vessels were subject to almost continuous harassment by little Japanese boats with samurai fighters on board. The stalemate would have continued for some time, were it not for a major tempest that struck the Tsushima Straits on August 15th. The two-day storm destroyed almost all of the Mongol fleet. The Japanese reported that over four thousand ships went down. Recent studies by marine archaeologists suggest that the ships built in Yangzhou were, in haste, improperly constructed and thus unable to withstand violent seas.

Kublai immediately sent out orders for the preparation of a third attack on Japan. These orders, however, were rescinded when the great khan became preoccupied with dissent within his empire. The most significant outcome of the two failed invasions of Japan was the now apparent fact that the Mongols were not, as previously believed, invincible.

The later years of Kublai's reign were distinguished by attempts to bolster his administration in areas of strategic importance. He appointed a Muslim governor for Yunnan in southern China in order to exercise tight control over the roads to Annam and Mian (Burma). The origins of the governor reveal the thinking of the great khan when it came to ensuring that his empire was properly managed by loyal administrators. Sayyid Ajall Shams al-Din Omar (1211-1279) was a Khwarezmian Muslim from Bukhara (in modern-day Uzbekistan). He had served in the army of Kublai and Möngke, and he had been instrumental in the conquest of the Kingdom of Dali in 1274. Sayyid excelled in Yunnan because, as an outsider, he was respected for his fair treatment of the people of the province. During his tenure, public works were improved with the institution of water conservation projects, irrigation works, and construction of terraces for gardens. Sayyid also built mosques, Confucian temples and schools, and a Buddhist monastery. After he died, his policies were continued by his sons. In short, under Sayyid, the Yuan province thrived, and the trade along paths leading to Southeast Asia expanded. While most of the trade between the West and Burma and Vietnam was a maritime enterprise, it is not unlikely that goods from the region traveled north by land to the ancient Silk Road and thence westward.

The kind of religious toleration and economic prosperity in Yunnan that was favored by Kublai did not exist for long in Beijing and other parts of the Mongol Empire. When Taoists in Beijing set a Buddhist monastery on fire in 1280, Kublai was forced to take action in what had been a long-simmering conflict. He ordered that copies of the Taoist Book of Barbarian Conversions be hunted down and destroyed. Although Kublai had previously made a similar prohibition against the book, it was not entirely effective, so he also ordered the destruction of all printing blocks that were used in making multiple copies of the book. Kublai's wrath fell heavily on uneducated and untrained ersatz Taoists who made their living offering services of divination, soothsaying, and other esoteric practices.

A further religious conflict erupted over the Muslim practice of halal, or permissible butchering. The practice was contrary to the Mongol custom of butchering animals, as they drained the blood prior to cutting apart the animal. It was these kinds of disputes that began to erupt in Kublai's court, which had been built so as to be all-inclusive with respect to religions. In the aftermath of the halal controversy, Muslims in the imperial administration were attacked by Buddhists and Taoists, and they fell victim to prejudice among the Chinese population who resented the authority of non-Chinese, regardless of their religion.

As Kublai aged, the question of what religion he preferred became more and more urgent. His fence-sitting stance on contending religions became less an attribute to be admired and more a thorn in his side. Kublai's appointment of his second son Zhenjin as his heir apparent in 1283 exacerbated the conflicts among religious leaders vying for power in the empire. Zhenjin was first educated by Confucian scholars before falling under the influence of a Tibetan Buddhist, Drogön Chögyal Phagpa, who is said to have written the book What One Should Know for the benefit of the young prince. It became a matter of urgency in the imperial court as to which religion Kublai's successor might favor. Nestorian Christians began to lose their authority, and Catholicism was a non-starter, so it was a toss-up whether Zhenjin would tend to be more sympathetic to Islam, Buddhism, Confucianism, or Taoism. Any currying of the favor of Zhenjin by religious leaders was not to bear fruit since Zhenjin died in 1286 at the age of 43.

Kublai's reign was thrust into turmoil in the years after the 1281 assassination of Ahmad Fanākati, who was one of his chief advisors on finance. It was never determined who perpetrated this act against the Mongol Muslim bureaucrat, but his replacements in the role provided his successor, the Chinese Lu Shizhong, a platform to exercise his prejudices. He instituted severe penalties for breaking the imperial monopoly on the production of liquor, which had the effect of angering Mongols and Chinese alike. Lu characterized the Mongol ruling class as "idle" and proposed that they be forced to raise herds on government land and turn over 80 percent of their profits to the imperial treasury. Among his solutions to the dwindling income of the treasury was to print more of the paper money that was already spurring on inflation. Lu was eventually accused by his abundant enemies of embezzlement and was thrown out of office and executed. His successor, a Uyghur or Tibetan named Sengge, was likewise unable to set the imperial finances in order and swiftly became hated inside and outside of the imperial court. He was also executed.

The dilemma facing Mongol rule in China is clearly stated by the authors of the History of the Yuan. The book, which is part of the Twenty-Four Histories of China, compiled in 1370 by the Ming Bureau of History, condemns the Mongols for a plethora of shortcomings. Generally, Mongols were unsuited to govern China because they were barbarians. Barbarians might conquer from the back of a horse, but they could never govern China because Chinese civilization was far too sophisticated and complicated for the Mongols to comprehend. Even when they put Chinese in positions of authority, such as Lu Shizhong, they were bound to fail because the foreigners were ultimately in control.

Kublai's troubles with religious disputes, the expression of ethnic and religious differences, and his failure to succeed in conquering Japan were compounded with his failure to force the capitulation of Southeast Asia. The great khan sent a letter to Vietnamese Emperor Trần Thánh Tông, demanding that he send treasure, scholars, doctors, astronomers, and other skilled workers, who Kublai would assimilate into the Mongol administration. Behind this was the Kublai's belief that the Vietnamese would supply troops for his continuing war against the Southern Song. This didn't happen, and Thánh Tông successfully postponed any visit he was commanded to make to Beijing. In fact, both he and his son succeeded in fending off Kublai's overtures to submit and his efforts to create a regime change in Vietnam. The final Mongol failure in Annam came with the success of General Trần Hưng Đạo in destroying a Mongol invasion fleet in 1285 and forcing ground troops out of his nation.

In the case of the annexation of Burma, the Mongols fared no better than they had in Vietnam. King Narathihapate, a colorful, bombastic despot, who was characterized by Marco Polo as a "puissant prince," dealt with the Mongol threat by testing the borders of his kingdom through attacking Mongol dependencies on the northern frontier. Having roundly wrested them from Mongol control, Narathihapate declined to figure out how to fend off the inevitable Mongol attack. Instead, he used the royal treasury and national manpower to build an enormous new temple, the Mingalezedi Pagoda, which may have been an effort to curry divine favor in the inevitable Mongol invasion. Narathihapate, however, was sorely mistaken for in 1277, the Mongols attacked under the leadership of the recently appointed governor of Yunnan, Nasir al-Din, the son of the highly competent Sayyid al-Din. Riding at breakneck speed down the mountains of Yunnan, the Mongol forces entered a land that Marco Polo said was full of "great woods abounding in elephants and unicorns and numbers of other wild beasts." When the forces of Nasir and King Narathihapate met, the Mongols faced an army unlike anything they had ever seen before. Burmese archers loosed volleys of arrows down from their elevated howdahs. The Mongol horsemen were unable to approach the phalanx of elephants as their horses took fright at the daunting animals. Hiding in a forest, Nasir's archers dismounted and shot shafts into the charging elephants, forcing Narathihapate's army to retreat. The king was forced to take poison by one of his sons, who was aghast at his father's loss of the capital and his commencement of negotiations to submit to Mongol rule. One of Narathihapate's sons attempted to claim the kingship and agreed to submit to the Mongols, but the kingdom was in disarray, with several factions vying for power. This complicated the Mongol cause as they were used to dealing with a single monarch, and making peace with a dubious pretender to the throne did not suit their cause. In effect, if the Mongols were to take Burma, they would have to wage war all over the country and subdue the rebellious viceroys one by one. A Mongol invasion in 1287 failed to subdue the disunified country, and in 1303, the Mongols finally left Burma to its own devices.

By 1280, though, Kublai was a sick man. He was overweight and crippled with gout, with both conditions being brought on by long-term overconsumption of alcohol. Marco Polo reported that the great khan traveled in a great wooden bastion "borne by four well-trained elephants, and over him was hoisted his standard." The traveling bastion was put to use when Kublai had to deal with a revolt in Manchuria, where another grandson of Genghis Khan, Nayan, claimed that Kublai had strayed too far from his Mongol roots. Kublai himself led a flotilla in 1287, and when his warriors disembarked, he led his massive army against Nayan. The great khan's entourage was "full of cross-bow men and archers," and he rode under his banner, "bearing the figures of the sun and moon." According to Marco Polo, the great khan's four elephants "were covered with very stout boiled hides, overlaid with cloths of silk and gold." Nayan, a Nestorian Christian, was defeated and executed.

Despite his failing health, Kublai continued his expansionist campaigns. An emissary to the Kingdom of Java in 1289 had his face branded and was summarily extradited from the island. It took some time for the great khan to learn of this humiliation, but when he did, he set the traditional Mongol system of retribution in motion. As if a branded and expelled ambassador wasn't enough to rile the Mongol court in Beijing, Kertanagara, the king of Java (r. 1268-1292), attacked and defeated the Mongol vassal state of Jumbi in Sumatra.

In 1292, a fleet sailed from China under orders to return Jumbi to Mongol control, defeat the Javanese, and turn the Kingdom of Java into a Mongol vassal state. As part of this flotilla was a group of ships that peeled away to India. It is supposed that on board one of these vessels was Marco Polo, who was delivering a Mongol princess bride to the Ilkhanate in Persia. Before the Mongols reached Java, Kertanagara was killed by one of his allies, and the dead king's son turned to the Mongols for assistance in avenging the death of his father. The rebel ally of the king of Java was defeated and killed, whereupon the dead king's son turned on his saviors, the Mongols, and declared his independence. Unwilling and unable to turn Java into a vassal state, the Mongol flotilla returned to China.

Early in 1294, the nearly eighty-year-old, obese, alcoholic Kublai died. In spite of his physical condition, he had done pretty well to have achieved this age. He was succeeded by his grandson, Temür, who served as the next great khan of the Mongol Empire until 1307. Under Temür, the Pagan Kingdom (Burma), the Tran Kingdom of Annam, and all southern Vietnam accepted the supremacy of the Mongols.

In the writing of history, much significance has been put on the travels of Marco Polo and his father and uncle. They were, in fact, not the initiators of European trade along the Silk Road. Before their trip and residence in Kublai's court, the route had been exploited by merchants from the Latin West. Determining exactly what this trade involved is difficult because the details of commercial enterprises by Europeans in the East were guarded as secrets by traders, who, in order to protect their advantage, kept their affairs private. When the Polos returned to Venice in 1295, their Italian compatriots had established trading businesses around the Black Sea, and the Genoese had established commercial activities in Persia. It was reported that around nine hundred Genoese were residents of Persia in the service of Arghun Khan, principally constructing galleys for Mongol trade in the Indian Ocean. European trade with Persia expanded when the pope forbade trade with the Mamluks of Egypt in the early 14th century. Venetian merchants also expanded their trade with the Persians during this time, setting up a consulate in Tabriz and establishing Dominican and Franciscan convents there. At the same time, Italian traders based in ports in the Black Sea penetrated central Asia, dealing in goods brought from China and India. It is recorded that in 1291, Peter of Lucalongo, who was perhaps a Venetian merchant, traveled from the Near East to southern China. In 1305, letters were sent to the West by a Latin missionary, reporting that a colony of Genoese and other Italian merchants had established depots at Zaiton on the Straits of Formosa. At the same time as the Europeans were exploring and trading along the Silk Road, they were developing trade by sea from China.

By the middle of the 14th century, the route along the Silk Road that was followed by the Polos was fairly well-known among Latin merchants. In the *Book of Descriptions of Countries and of Measures Employed in Business*, which was written by a Florentine trader, Francesco Balducci Pegolotti, in about 1343, the author said that the road from Persia to China "is quite safe both by day and by night." But, he warns, if a trader is on the road when the overlord dies, "in the interval sometimes a disorder occurs against the Franks and other foreigners—they call 'Franks' all Christians of countries from the Byzantine Empire westwards—and the road is not safe until the new lord is sent for who is to reign after the one who died."

This was a bit of deception, as it was based on second-hand knowledge. In fact, traveling the Silk Road was a daunting affair. The challenges of the central Asia steppes, deserts, and mountains were, however, worth the effort for traders who acquired ginger, sugar, and rhubarb, items which were all prized in Europe as much as silk. The most sought-after silk was that produced in Turkestan. That overland trade with China was extensive by the mid-14th century is indicated by the discovery of two Christian tombstones in Yangzhou (in China's Jiangsu province). They are dated in Gothic lettering and are for the children of a Genoese merchant who died in 1342 and 1344. Trade must have been settled enough for Latin merchants to bring along family members as they were setting up businesses in China.

Conclusion: The Decline of Trade Along the Silk Road

After the death of Kublai Khan in 1294, the Mongol Empire, which included Yuan China, was led by his grandson, Temür Khan. He maintained Mongol policies and worked to discharge the debts of his father for military campaigns, particularly those against Vietnam. Temür also appointed court officials from among several ethnic groups and religions, including individuals of Tibetan and Khwarezmian origins. Although Confucianism was the court religion, officials included Muslims, Buddhists, Taoists, and Christians. He established peace with breakaway khanates, including bringing the Golden Horde in the West under his control. Temür Khan ended Mongol expansion in the south and east, ceasing to demand the complete submission of Japan, Burma, and Đại Việt (Vietnam).

Despite Temür Khan's reforms, his reign marks the beginning of the slow collapse of the Mongol-led Yuan dynasty in China and the larger Mongol Empire as a whole. A number of factors played a role in this. The small number of Mongols in the administration of vassal states allowed unrest to grow unchecked. These rebellious leaders of various ethnicities, situated anywhere from China to the Near East, fractured the Mongol Empire, resulting in the formation of independent states that were freed from their subservience to the central government in Beijing. The rise of non-Mongol states along the Silk Road made travel and navigating complex and different trade regulations extremely difficult. In China itself, the remnants of the Mongol ruling class were forced to retreat to their traditional homeland, where their society had devolved into the kind of quasi-feudalism similar to that under Genghis Khan.

The last of the Mongol emperors of China, Toghon Temür Khan (r. 1333-1368) was a dissolute character, much like Roman Emperor Caligula. He preferred sexual orgies to administration, and so, the split between the four parts of the Mongol Empire—China (with Mongolia, Korea, and Tibet), central Asia, the Ilkhanate in western Asia, and the Golden Horde in Russia—became permanent.

What was to become the most powerful empire in the years of lessening Mongol control was founded in Turco-Mongol Persia by Timur or Tamerlane (r. 1370-1405) in Iran and central Asia. Timur's ethnicity was distinctly not Mongol, but he fashioned himself as a warlord in the tradition of Genghis Khan. His military successes in Persia, central Asia, India, Armenia, Georgia, and Syria indicate that he had the military ability and the means to be a successful emulator of Genghis Khan. While Timur was expanding his empire in the West, in China, the first of the Ming emperors were ridding the country of the remnants of Yuan loyalists. In 1394, the Ming emperor was in a position where he could write boldly to Timur, making the claim that Timur himself was subject to Ming authority. After making an alliance with the Mongols living in Mongolia, Timur prepared to attack Ming China. Before reaching the border of China, he died. His body was embalmed and taken back to Samarkand to be interred in a tomb, known as the Gur-e Amir, which still stands today.

The interruption of the land trade route from China to the West by the rise of Timur in the 14th century was more than made up for by the expansion in maritime trade between the East and West. Seaborne exploration and trade in China date back to the creation of a navy in the period of the Qin dynasty (221-206 BCE), and based on the excavation of a shipyard in Guangzhou, maritime activity was quite sophisticated in the early Han dynasty (201 BCE-220 CE). The coastline of the South China Sea seems to have been the extent of early Chinese seaborne trade. Chinese merchants sailed into the Indian Ocean from the late 2nd century BCE and are said to have traveled as far as Ethiopia. Travel to and from India was commonplace by the 7th century, as Chinese vessels would often sail to the Red Sea and up the Euphrates River in modern-day Iraq.

Chinese seaborne mercantilism changed in the 15th century during the period of the explorations of Zheng He, who led seven expeditions into the Indian Ocean under orders from the Yongle Emperor, the third emperor of the Ming Dynasty. Zheng He's voyages were aboard ships that were larger than had ever been constructed in China. Some of his vessels, which were made to carry treasure back to China, may have measured as much as 400 feet long and 170 feet wide. On his first voyage, which lasted from 1405 to 1407, Zheng He reached Calcutta. In subsequent journeys, he explored as far as the coast of Africa. The strange things he brought back to China—animals, art, and manufactured goods—provided the impetus for the growth of vast maritime trading enterprises.

In the wake of Zheng He's voyages, the East/West maritime trade between China, Indochina, India, Africa, and Persia expanded to such an extent that it replaced the arduous land route of the Silk Road. Shortly after Zheng He explored maritime routes to the West, Europeans, principally Spanish and Portuguese explorers, set out to discover maritime routes to the East, where they knew goods sought after in European markets could be obtained. The Portuguese sailor Bartolomeu Dias, who lived from 1450 to 1500, reached the Cape of Good Hope and determined that the east coast of Africa was accessible by ship. He was followed by Vasco da Gama, who lived from around 1460 to 1524 and who rounded the tip of Africa and reached India. By opening up maritime trade to the East, the Europeans were able to dispense with the services of Arab intermediaries. This led to the opening up of longer trade routes to the Far East, including China and the Pacific Islands.

It was in the Age of Discovery (the early 15th century to the mid-17th century) that alternative trade routes between the East and the West replaced the Silk Road. The transporting of goods by sea was much cheaper and quicker than overland transport. Larger quantities of goods could also be moved with greater reliability, as they were subject only to the dangers of the sea, which were minimal compared to the dangers of marauders and greedy upstart ethnic regimes that infested the Silk Road. The old Silk Road did not fall into complete disuse as the traditional intercommunity trade continues to exist up to the present day.

If you enjoyed this book, then I'd really appreciate it if you would post a short review on Amazon. I read all the reviews myself so that I can continue to provide books that people want.

Here's another book by Captivating History that you might be interested in

Further Reading

Christopher Beckwith, *Empires of the Silk Road: A History of Central Eurasia from the Bronze Age to the Present* (Princeton: Princeton University Press, 2009)

Peter Hopkirk, *Foreign Devils on the Silk Road: The Search for the Lost Cities and Treasures of Chinese Central Asia* (London: Murray, 1980)

John Man, *Genghis Khan: Life, Death and Resurrection* (New York: Thomas Dunne Books, 2004)

Jonathan Clements, *A Brief History of Khublai Khan: Lord of Xanadu, Emperor of China* (London: Robinson, 2010).